Leaders on Leadership: The College Presidency

James L. Fisher, *Editor*
President Emeritus, CASE

Martha W. Tack, *Editor*
Bowling Green State University

NEW DIRECTIONS FOR HIGHER EDUCATION
MARTIN KRAMER, *Editor-in-Chief*
University of California, Berkeley

Number 61, Spring 1988

Paperback sourcebooks in
The Jossey-Bass Higher Education Series

Jossey-Bass Inc., Publishers
San Francisco • London

James L. Fisher, Martha W. Tack (eds.).
Leaders on Leadership: The College Presidency.
New Directions for Higher Education, no. 61.
Volume XVI, number 1.
San Francisco: Jossey-Bass, 1988.

New Directions for Higher Education
Martin Kramer, *Editor-in-Chief*

New Directions for Higher Education is published quarterly
by Jossey-Bass Inc., Publishers (publication number USPS
990-880). *New Directions* is numbered sequentially—please
order extra copies by sequential number. The volume and issue
numbers above are included for the convenience of libraries.
Second-class postage paid at San Francisco, California, and at
additional mailing offices. POSTMASTER: Send address changes to
Jossey-Bass Inc., Publishers, 350 Sansome Street, San Francisco,
California 94104.

Editorial correspondence should be sent to the Editor-in-Chief,
Martin Kramer, 2807 Shasta Road, Berkeley, California 94708.

Library of Congress Catalog Card Number LC 85-644752

International Standard Serial Number ISSN 0271-0560

International Standard Book Number ISBN 1-55542-918-1

Cover art by WILLI BAUM

Manufactured in the United States of America. Printed on acid-free paper.

Ordering Information

The paperback sourcebooks listed below are published quarterly and can be ordered either by subscription or single copy.

Subscriptions cost $48.00 per year for institutions, agencies, and libraries. Individuals can subscribe at the special rate of $36.00 per year *if payment is by personal check.* (Note that the full rate of $48.00 applies if payment is by institutional check, even if the subscription is designated for an individual.) Standing orders are accepted.

Single copies are available at $11.95 when payment accompanies order. (California, New Jersey, New York, and Washington, D.C., residents please include appropriate sales tax.) For billed orders, cost per copy is $11.95 plus postage and handling.

Substantial discounts are offered to organizations and individuals wishing to purchase bulk quantities of Jossey-Bass sourcebooks. Please inquire.

Please note that these prices are for the calendar year 1988 and are subject to change without notice. Also, some titles may be out of print and therefore not available for sale.

To ensure correct and prompt delivery, all orders must give either the *name of an individual* or an *official purchase order number.* Please submit your order as follows:

Subscriptions: specify series and year subscription is to begin.
Single Copies: specify sourcebook code (such as, HE1) and first two words of title.

Mail orders for United States and Possessions, Australia, New Zealand, Canada, Latin America, and Japan to:
> Jossey-Bass Inc., Publishers
> 350 Sansome Street
> San Francisco, California 94104

Mail orders for all other parts of the world to:
> Jossey-Bass Limited
> 28 Banner Street
> London EC1Y 8QE

New Directions for Higher Education Series
Martin Kramer, *Editor-in-Chief*

Contents

Editors' Notes

Who in his or her right mind wants to be a college president? This question is typically raised when people get together to talk about the state of affairs in higher education today. Without a doubt, the existing social and fiscal environment is not conducive to creative progress: College and university presidents have to deal not only with public assaults on the curriculum, an aging faculty, a physically deteriorating campus, and reduced funding, but also with the internal stress of knowing that they could do so much more if others would just let them.

Maybe we have brought this situation on ourselves because of our own shortsightedness or the constraints we create for ourselves. We moan about the problems of diminished funding and seem unable to excite the public about our high purpose. We are agitated when Joe and Janet Q. Public point a finger at colleges and universities as the culprits when teachers cannot teach and students cannot read; but we want public support for increased taxes and we want private funds. We call for someone to lead us, but we want to tell our leaders exactly how to do it and what range of decisions we will accept. In addition, we want the president to be the key educational leader for the institution, as well as a fundraiser, a scholar, a community relations expert. . . . and the list goes on.

We read weekly in the *Chronicle of Higher Education* about yet another president whose contract was not renewed or one who resigned because of health problems. Needless to say, the situation is not ideal for the care and feeding of an enthusiastic, energetic, strong-willed, decisive president. Those who have the potential to be extremely successful presidents often do not consider the job because of its no-win, personally destructive image. Yet without good, dedicated leaders, higher education will not flourish.

Unquestionably, a few effective chief executive officers have emerged in the recent past, giving us a glimmer of hope that all is not lost. We are fortunate that eighteen of these effective leaders agreed to work with us in the compilation of this sourcebook and in so doing have provided invaluable insight into the nature of leadership today, especially from the vantage point of a college or university president. While certainly reflecting the problems and issues associated with the presidential position, the tone of these manuscripts is upbeat, indicating that being a president is exciting, challenging, rewarding work. Clearly, the president's impact on a college or a university is significant, either ensuring its vitality or contributing to its demise. Therefore, we need to know more about the factors that influence effective presidential leadership.

1

2

Vision

A prerequisite for success in the presidency is the ability to dream dreams that come true. Without a doubt, the president must be able to articulate a clear and realizable vision for the institution and be able to motivate others to work for that cause. This vision must reflect some of the traditions and history of the institution, but it must also be futuristic and challenging to those who will be called on to help achieve it. The president must be like a broken record, consistently repeating the same message to different groups, even in the face of cynicism on the part of constituents who disagree or are too tired to care.

Courage

The effective president is unabashedly confident and unafraid to think differently. Indeed, he or she must frequently stand alone in the quest for quality and the realization of the vision. Certainly, the president must give consistent support to faculty, students, and staff as they seek new programs and methods for educating our citizens, yet he or she must always be the "fly in the ointment," constantly stirring things up and encouraging people to try new things, rather than be satisfied with the status quo.

The president must also have the courage to leave the job when, for whatever reason, his or her ability to be effective has been compromised. This simply means that the effective president must be secure enough to resign from the position with dignity and grace, rather than be forced out of office. Clearly, the president must want to be the chief executive officer, but he or she must not need to be.

A Take-Charge Attitude

A president cannot sit back and wait for change but must capitalize on the opportunities presented and even create a few. Thus, the president must be a risk taker, one who studies the situation carefully (but not too long to lose the opportunity) and takes decisive action. Naturally, the effective president enjoys saying yes but does not hesitate to say no when the situation warrants it. Indeed, the president must be a renegade, challenging the bureaucracy and braving unpopularity to build a top-quality, responsive institution.

The effective president always keeps a close rein on the educational process, in terms of both what is being taught and who is teaching it. Thus, the effective president walks a tightrope. Given the fact that the president cannot do everything, he or she must delegate authority to others. Nevertheless, the chief executive cannot delegate responsibility, for he or she is the one ultimately accountable for results.

Commitment

Above all, the president must believe in the importance of higher education and the impact it can have on society at large. Realistically, those who are successful want to be presidents because they care, not because they want what little money, power, or prestige may be awarded. The job is demanding and affects every aspect of the president's life; therefore, the president must be willing to give all his or her time and energy to the achievement of the cause. Only those who are excited about learning and discovery, who are energized by the challenge of solving the seemingly unsolvable problem, and who have the physical stamina to work nearly twenty-four hours a day should consider the presidency. In short, the effective president devotes his or her life to making a positive difference in the world through the entity known as higher education.

Personal Style

Effective presidents are rather easy to identify. They are the ones you remember after having met them only once. They captivate you with their charm and their positive attitudes toward life, excite you about your own potential, and make you want to work hard to achieve the dream in which they so strongly believe. On first meeting them, you feel that you have known them all your life, but on reflection, you realize that you know much more about them professionally than personally, even though you so avidly admire them. They are open-minded and capable of being persuaded to change a position, but they are doggedly persistent in achieving their goals. They demand honesty and loyalty—not loyalty to themselves personally, but to the accomplishment of goals. They do not understand and will not tolerate lack of commitment or mediocre performance on the part of those associated with them. They work hard, and they expect others to do the same.

The eighteen presidents who have shared their wisdom and understanding with us have plugged one hole in the protective armor of chief executive officers. Instead of referring to it as unusually difficult and negative, these presidents have focused on the numerous opportunities, challenges, and satisfactions associated with the presidency. Perhaps this is why they have been so successful as leaders.

Effective presidents will lead, if we let them. We can and must restore the presidency to prominence in higher education. We can begin this restoration process by training, selecting, nurturing, supporting, and rewarding effective leaders. We must educate good people, perhaps through the apprenticeship method, to handle the demands of the position. We must select people who fit the institution, in terms of vision and expectations, and who are strong, decisive leaders. We must support

4

and nurture those who are willing to give their lives to the challenge of building a better future for America through education. We must reward effectiveness by celebrating successes, debunking myths, and continuing to determine what makes the big difference in whether one is an effective president. We must also share the secrets of success once we know what they are.

Effective presidents are strong-willed, committed, charismatic individuals working in institutions where people understand the importance of good leadership. We need more of them. If we do not do something, the effective presidential species may become extinct. If we protect and assist these people, while encouraging others to follow in their footsteps, we may be able to increase their numbers. We believe this sourcebook, which contains some exceptionally good advice from masters of the art, is one step in the right direction.

James L. Fisher
Martha W. Tack
Editors

James L. Fisher is president emeritus of the Council for Advancement and Support of Education and president emeritus of Towson State University. He is the author of Power of the Presidency *(1984) and coauthor (with Tack and Wheeler) of* The Effective College President *(1988).*

Martha W. Tack is professor of educational administration and supervision at Bowling Green State University. She has served in a variety of administrative positions in higher education, including assistant to the president and American Council on Education Intern at the University of Alabama, Tuscaloosa. She is coauthor (with Fisher and Wheeler) of The Effective College President *(1988).*

*A leader needs a clear and challenging vision, a magic with
words, the ability to motivate others, the courage to stay
on course, and the persistence not to lose hope.*

Academic Leadership

Theodore M. Hesburgh

Anyone who has been reading John Gardner's series of essays will agree
that leadership is very complicated as a concept and as a reality. I shall
not even try to distinguish leadership from management, administration,
or other cognate ideas and concepts. It is difficult enough to see leadership as a discrete idea, and even then one has the new problem of distin-
guishing the different kinds of leadership. Obviously, academic leadership
is not the same as business or military leadership; that is probably why
business leaders and generals do not usually make very good university
or college presidents. The French have a great philosophical saying:
Distinguer pour comprende (distinguish to understand). If it is possible to
establish a few clear characteristics of academic leadership, we may be
able to understand it better.

My experience has been uniquely in a major Catholic university,
and so my analysis must be understood and evaluated in that context; I
have no other. (I have tried to exercise leadership in other contexts—
government and church activities—but those worlds often required other
kinds of leadership.) Staying, then, with specifically academic leadership,
and beginning the analysis on the highest level of generality, my first
observation is that there is no leadership without vision. (Two biblical
thoughts come immediately to mind: "Without vision, the people perish"
and "Who will follow the uncertain trumpet?") The vision, of course,
must be specific to the area of leadership: It does not help the university

J. L. Fisher and M. W. Tack (eds.). *Leaders on Leadership: The College Presidency.*
New Directions for Higher Education, no. 61. San Francisco: Jossey-Bass, Spring 1988.

if the president knows how to end the war in Central America but is fuzzy about what to do about emphasizing the humanities in the university curriculum.

It is not enough to have a vision of sorts, somewhat muddled. The leader must know clearly what he or she wants to achieve and, even more important, must have the ability to articulate the vision in equally clear words and images.

Even clarity does not suffice, however. We have all known leaders who were clear but unenthusiastic. Somehow the leader must join clarity of mind to warmth of heart to make his or her vision not only come to life but also be espoused by all those people who are essential to realizing that vision.

My second observation is that such persons do not just materialize on the spot; they must be selected and convinced to serve. Some potential leaders lack self-confidence and self-assurance; they will never be true leaders. The true leader is not threatened by searching out and appointing a team of persons who may be older, more experienced, more competent in the area where they are most needed, more attractive, and even more personable than the leader is. Quite the contrary: He or she seeks out the most competent and persuades them to join in the exciting endeavor. The leader promises them a free field of creative activity, makes them feel needed, and welcomes them as essential to the vision. He or she does not try to second-guess them or do their work for them. Once they have been enlisted as members of the team, the leader brings them together and praises them individually for what they bring to the group and to the total endeavor. Then he or she outlines the vision and enlists their enthusiastic support to achieve it.

The sequence is important: clear vision (realistic and realizable), persuasion and enlistment of essential support persons, enthusiastic articulation of the vision to enlist the support of the whole team, an atmosphere of reasonable autonomy, and consensus on plans. Is this all there is to leadership? Hardly—this is only the beginning. A vision can quickly fade if it is not enthusiastically reiterated. The vision also needs constant new expression. Moreover, there are many different components of a total vision—especially that of a great university—and these must be ordered realistically, because the parts make up the whole. There is nothing wrong with achieving a vision sequentially and in parts; in fact, there is no other way to do it.

When I first became president of the University of Notre Dame, I knew fundamentally that to have a great university, we needed a great faculty, a great student body, more than twice the academic facilities we did have, and a library six times greater. This could all be translated into a budget twenty times larger, with greatly increased faculty salaries and better fringe benefits; scholarships for more than half the students; better laboratories and more computers; more dormitories and dining facilities; better maintenance; a much larger power plant; and, above all, an endowment at least fifty times larger than what we had.

Obviously, a vision like this one cannot all be realized at once. The campaign is conducted on many fronts, and leadership involves encouraging the subsidiary leaders of each line of endeavor and holding out hope for each of them as they respect current priorities. The leader never loses sight of the total vision, even though he or she is always pressing forward on the particular front where immediate progress is possible. Somehow—with a lot of luck, coordinated efforts, and movement where movement is possible—the whole dream begins to take shape, and the institution moves forward toward the whole, organic, unified goal of total excellence. This movement will not happen unless the leader holds the torch high, especially during dark days and times of frustrated hopes. He or she cannot afford to be discouraged when everyone else is. The leader cannot allow overemphasis on one aspect of the institution (like athletics) to pervert and fracture the total vision.

Courage is needed for the leader to admit having picked the wrong person for a particular part of the vision. The leader needs to replace that person, without destroying him or her. The leader also needs patience to cope with inevitable blame for the mistakes of others. The leader must swallow that blame without recrimination: He or she is, after all, in charge.

The true leader sustains the morale of the team by a variety of sensitive actions. For example, the leader will see that people get full credit for the good they do (even when what they do is the leader's idea in the first place). One can get a lot accomplished if one does not care who gets the credit. The true leader often gets little praise along the way; he or she is too busy praising others. When the total task is completed, there will be praise enough for all.

The leader is also sensitive to the mental, physical, and spiritual health of coworkers. The leader does not just use people; he or she cares for them and their marriages, their families, and their careers. He or she is alert to burnout and exhaustion and heads it off before it happens, even though it may cost a few thousand dollars to provide an unexpected but much needed vacation.

While the leader is caring for others, often enough no one is caring for him or her. Leadership is admittedly a lonely task, not for the person without self-discipline, and not for one requiring constant praise and moral support. The leader gives these; he or she cannot count on getting them. For a thousand persons the leader thanks and praises, he or she may be thanked and praised only a few times. No matter: The leader's task is to realize the vision in its totality; his or her reward is to see that happen.

8

Leadership may involve moments of sudden crisis; more generally, it involves years and persistence. In the university, leadership consists of persuading, rather than ordering with authority. Moral leadership requires one to jump first when courage is required and to stay until last when danger lurks. In a way, leadership is the worst of all worlds, but it is also the best. Leaders are few, and the rewards are internal.

If all this is so, why do people volunteer or allow themselves to be chosen as leaders? I do not know. I suspect that there is an inner calling, a vision that, if accomplished, will leave this a better world. I happen to believe that in the case of something beyond the material and transitory—a spiritual vision, whether for peace, human rights, an end to human hunger and misery, or even a great Catholic university—there is also a divine calling. Grace can be denied but often is not, because the vision beckons even more insistently and the stakes are higher in the long run.

In summary, then, a leader needs a clear and challenging vision, a magic with words, the ability to motivate others, the courage to stay on course, the persistence not to lose hope or cease to inspire it, and the humility to share what glory there is in success.

One last word: The leader should not take himself or herself too seriously. He or she should maintain a sense of humor. Seeing what is comic, even in ourselves, is the best antidote to pomposity and pride.

Reverend Theodore M. Hesburgh, C.S.C., is president emeritus of the University of Notre Dame, having served as the institution's chief executive officer from 1952–1987.

Leaders today must be deeply knowledgeable about the past,
widely informed about the present, and willing to substitute
the common good for their own.

On Leadership

David Pierpont Gardner

Ralph Waldo Emerson, speaking of leadership, argued, "An institution
is the lengthened shadow of one man." He was half right. Many institutions have indeed sprung from seeds planted by one uniquely creative
individual, but leadership itself is far broader than that and far more
complex, whether one speaks of education or politics or any other sphere
of human endeavor, including leadership of a college or a university. In
America, it seems to me, the quintessential illustration of the nature and
dynamics of leadership is the framing of the U.S. Constitution. Anyone
interested in what it takes to be a leader can profit from that splendid
example.

The Constitution, which we rightly celebrate as an authentic
human triumph, was composed by a handful of men living at the western
fringe of European civilization. Franklin and Madison, Hamilton and
Jay, together with their cosigners in Philadelphia two hundred years ago,
fashioned America's most creative and singularly brilliant expression of
global leadership. This document both founded a nation and provided
an ensign for a restive and weary world to follow. It was a radical act,
subverting the old order and illuminating the one to come. The world
has never been the same since. How did the genius of this document
come about?

The framers of the Constitution were counted among the political,
social, intellectual, military, agricultural, and business leaders of what

J. L. Fisher and M. W. Tack (eds.). *Leaders on Leadership: The College Presidency.*
New Directions for Higher Education, no. 61. San Francisco: Jossey-Bass, Spring 1988.

had been the colonies. In this sense, they were leaders in the most familiar and conventional of ways, but they were more than that. They brought to their task a disciplined, informed, and sophisticated appreciation of their culture and of the civilization to which they belonged. They possessed not a parochial but a universal view of the world and their place in it. *The Federalist*, for example, reflects the authors' acquaintance with ancient and modern history; it also reflects, in its often stunning prose, Hamilton's love of literature, Madison's sophisticated and almost uncanny comprehension of political philosophy and theory, and Jay's grasp of the law and its civilizing role.

These men were prepared for their task and free to perform it. They were prepared because of the breadth, depth, and richness of their education and training. They were free because of the American Revolution, which at once liberated this new land and, in the Declaration of Independence and the Constitution, gave expression to the political thought, theories, and philosophy of eighteenth-century Europe, but within the less-fettered confines of an expanding New World.

We are living two hundred years later, of course, and in a world far different from that of the founders of our nation, when Washington admonished his country to remain free of foreign entanglements. American leaders today confront a world almost completely unlike Washington's; but, remarkably, we are still governed under the document signed in Philadelphia by America's first leaders. They possessed a sense of the forces that were shaping their culture and their civilization; indeed, they manifested an almost magical comprehension of their times. How can we today capture for our own times the kind of leadership the founders brought to theirs?

We will surely not do so merely by the crass use of rhetoric, symbols, images, or impressions masquerading for meaning and substance. We will not do so with riskless solutions or timid initiatives. We will not do so acting out of pure self-interest or personal aggrandizement. We will not do so by a disproportionate reliance on coercion or force of arms or the power of money. We will not do so by an opportunism that seeks to excuse or otherwise justify our ignorance of our own past or of the world as it is shaped and formed by forces, events, and ideas whose significance we do not comprehend. Tactical and temporary gain or advantage may be derived from such means or motives, but the attainment of strategic and lasting objectives requires leadership that is more than illusory and that does more than merely accommodate pressures for short-term solutions from single-interest pressure groups.

Such leadership is not easily nurtured in today's America. We live in a society that tends to encourage the demand for daily answers and facile solutions, where bumper stickers and turns of phrase on the evening news substitute for discussion and are mistaken for commentary and communication, where appearance overpowers reason, and where images and manipulations of symbols not only are big business but even more often are substitutes for the message.

We underestimate the average citizen's intelligence and ability. We undervalue his or her common sense. We underuse the talent, skill, and energy of our dynamic society. In short, we have somehow come to believe that top-down solutions are preferable to bottom-up ones. The Constitution, together with its amendments, vested the nation's sovereignty and security in the people. Contemporary leaders, no less than their counterparts two centuries ago, should have recourse to the precepts and principles that framed our nation and infused it with the liberating and energizing proposition that the people ought to control their government, not the reverse.

In 1983, the members of the National Commission on Excellence in Education decided to test the point I have just made. The commission had been asked by the government to prepare a report on the quality of schooling in America. We did so, but it was a report addressed not so much to the government as to the American people, in the form of an open letter. We titled it *A Nation at Risk.*

Our approach was straightforward: If what we had to say about the nation's schools made sense to the average citizen, then things would happen, and government would respond; and if the report made sense to the government but not to the people, then little would happen. Thus, we wrote our open letter to the American people in plain English. We said no more than we needed to say for the main points to be made. We defined the problem, offered possible solutions, made clear why the subject was important to the nation and its future, and invited a response fitted to the interest and circumstances of the reader.

This report of thirty-six pages has been reprinted in over thirteen million copies. It has provoked the most searching examination of the quality of schooling in America in more than twenty-five years and has sparked an educational reform movement, both here and abroad, that remains remarkably robust.

Nevertheless, the mere acts of unlocking the door, opening it for citizens' involvement, and welcoming new ideas cannot fully define the responsibility of leaders. Like the founders, leaders today must be both prepared and free to perform their role. By *prepared*, I mean deeply knowledgeable about the past, widely informed about the present, and capable of understanding and influencing change; and by *free*, I mean willing to substitute the common good for their own.

We live in a shrinking world, more interdependent and complex than the early leaders of our nation could possibly have envisioned. For example, the industrial and scientific revolutions, the advancement of technology, the industrialization of labor—what the historian and phi-

12

losopher Hichem Djait refers to as the forces of modernity—are confronting and challenging the world's great civilizations more than those civilizations are confronting and challenging one another. As Djait (1985) argues, we tend to confuse these forces of modernity with the spread of Western culture. According to Djait, however, that is a provincial view; instead, "the pattern emerging is not a confrontation between civilizations but of each one with modernity" (pp. 172, 173). Only our mutual incomprehension leads us to confuse the forces of modernity with what is thought to be the expansion of Western civilization.

How can we, bounded by great oceans to our east and west and by our own ignorance to our south, prepare and equip our leaders with a capacity to surmount the profound insularity of our own country and culture? The answer, of course, is principally by means of education; but, given our conventions and habits, this is no easy task, since we value so little the study of foreign languages, history, philosophy, geography, other civilizations and cultures, art, and the richness of our own language in both oral and written form. In this respect, our universities could do a much better job than they do. Why, for example, is there only one school of international relations in the United States that looks west to the nations of the Pacific, rather than east to Europe? Japan, after all, is not California's far east, but rather its near west. As Thomas Jefferson warned almost two hundred years ago, "If a nation expects to be ignorant and free, in a state of civilization, it expects what never was and never will be."

Our tendency is falsely to assume that commitment, desire, and raw intelligence will prove equal to the task of leadership today. They will not. Those attributes were essential for the authors of our Constitution to possess, as they are today for the nation's leaders; but, in the end, what the founders wrote was what counted, and what they wrote was drawn from a fund of knowledge, incisively engaged and brilliantly expressed, sweeping and strategic in its scope and significance, suited not just for their time, but for ours as well.

Reference

Djait, H. *Europe and Islam.* Los Angeles: University of California Press, 1985.

David Pierpont Gardner is president of the University of California. He chaired the National Commission on Excellence in Education, whose 1983 report, A Nation at Risk, *helped spark a national effort to improve schooling in America.*

An effective university president must be first, foremost, and always an educator.

Should College Presidents Be Educators?

John Silber

Colleges and universities, unlike most institutions of similar complexity, are subject to strong centrifugal forces. In a profit-making institution, the "bottom line" provides a basic guide for action, a guide lacking in the academy. Colleges and universities, suffused (and properly so) by individualism, with a high degree of autonomy needed by faculty and students alike, require leadership at the top, to an exceptional extent. Leadership must be exercised not through simple authority but through rational persuasion.

If we survey the exercise of academic leadership in this country, we can make a number of generalizations. Although far from universal, they are based on more than isolated cases. It is a sad fact, but from the day they take office, college presidents may be undone simply because of their terror of losing that office. Out of fear, they fail to develop standards, to set priorities and objectives—in short, to exercise leadership. By seeking approval from all their many constituencies, they frequently pursue vacillating courses harmful to their institutions and themselves. They stay in office by doing as little as possible and trying to camouflage their lack of ideas, educational policies, or courage as profound respect for faculty autonomy and deep sensitivity to student needs.

J. L. Fisher and M. W. Tack (eds.). *Leaders on Leadership: The College Presidency.*
New Directions for Higher Education, no. 61. San Francisco: Jossey-Bass, Spring 1988.

There are, of course, college presidents who have little or no academic background, who have no educational ideas, and who have neither plans for the future of their institutions nor any notion of what should be expected of students. It is quite natural that such administrators delegate everything to the faculty and students; because of their lack of minimal qualifications, they clearly should never have been appointed in the first place.

A corollary must also be noted: An administrator may lose his or her job precisely because he or she has been a leader and has performed exceedingly well. Some reforms, for example, cannot be effected without jeopardizing the reformer. While it is no great honor to be fired from a post, there may be good and sufficient reasons for congratulating one who is willing to use the full powers of the presidential office to accomplish worthy goals, without compromise or concern for his or her own future. In short, the genuine exercise of leadership may lead to a president's removal, and his or her undoing may be a good index of just how much he or she has done.

These observations apply not only to college presidents but also to leaders of many other types of institutions. Effective university presidents in particular, however, must be first, foremost, and always educators. Today some university presidents and chancellors view themselves as mere managers, with no special competence as educators. Conspicuous failures in administration during the 1960s and the 1970s led some boards of trustees and politicians to entrust the educational enterprise to lawyers and professional managers, rather than to educators with administrative ability. Moreover, rather than rely on their own experience and competence, trustees increasingly delegate the selection process to headhunting firms dominated by managerial consultants, who will almost invariably recommend managers, not leaders.

My point is not that deans or presidents must always be recruited from academic ranks; I acknowledge the possibility of a Grandma Moses of higher education. If a president of nonacademic background succeeds, however, it will be because he or she has the native genius of a folk educator, rather than mere managerial skills. If a president of academic background does not lead—if he or she merely fills the post and fails to realize its full educational potential, that is, the normative requirements of the office—he or she is substantially worse than a manager whose ignorance and innocence are extenuating factors.

The college president who is truly an educator will not leave crucial decisions about tenure and the retention of deans and faculty solely to others. The college president who fails to read the dossiers of prospective candidates for tenure and to review carefully each case fails to meet his or her most important responsibilities. He or she relies instead on deans, departmental chairs, or committees, none of whom can be held to account for the well-being of the university as a whole or for making sure that the resources of the university are used in the most effective ways.

Of course, no college president can be a universal expert. On what basis, then, does a president—a linguist, say, or a historian—evaluate a candidate for an appointment in physics? The recommendation for appointment reaches the president through the department. Recommendations include the opinions of the candidate's colleagues, of the departmental chair, and of the dean. The president must first assess the value of their opinions. How good are these colleagues who are making the recommendations? Are there any outstanding physicists among them? Has the quality of their judgment been proved in the past? Are they prejudiced by personal relationships with the candidate? Is there an intellectual or personal agenda that may interfere with their judgments? To assess the quality of a department's judgments, a college president will often need to call on outside experts who have no links to the department or to the candidates involved. For example, as dean of arts and sciences at the University of Texas, I used to call on John Wheeler, then a professor at Princeton, whenever an important decision with regard to an appointment in physics arose. Wheeler, if he knew the candidate's work, would provide an assessment. If he did not, he would suggest the names of the two or three most outstanding physicists in the candidate's particular field. (On one occasion, a department and its chair recommended a man as being one of the two best in his field. When I consulted outside experts, that opinion was confirmed, but one expert asked, "Did you know there are only two people working in this field? In the opinion of the leading authorities, the field is a dead end.")

As a president gains confidence that departmental chairs, deans, and other administrators are making sound independent assessments, as he or she finds administrators who allocate the funds of the university as if the money were their own, living up to the responsibility involved in a decision to invest as much as $3 million in a single tenured position, he or she may then attenuate individual involvement. When doubts remain, however, the president must maintain crucial involvement. It is the president's responsibility to certify to the board of trustees that a candidate has been properly assessed. Whenever there is serious doubt, the president must have the courage to veto an appointment.

When assessing candidates in fields closely related to his or her own, a president should provide first-hand corrective or collaborative judgments. I once reviewed for tenure a distinguished social scientist who had come highly recommended. Members of his department and outside reviewers agreed that he was a leader in his field; there was not a single negative judgment. On reading the man's work, however, I found his research methodology suspect. For example, in an attempt to establish the most obscene words in the English language, he had provided a list and asked experimental subjects to rank the words from most to least obscene. He failed, however, to ask his respondents whether they knew the meaning of the words on the list. I doubt that anyone would have known the meaning of more than two-thirds of them. "Jabberwocky," had it been on this social scientist's list, could have been proved by this "empirical methodology" to be the dirtiest word in the English language.

A president who is truly a leader and an educator does not buy the clichés of his or her trade—for instance, the notion that a university with a ten-to-one student-teacher ratio is better than a university with a twenty-to-one ratio. A president who truly understands the process of education knows that ideal student-teacher ratios vary according to subject matter and faculty talents. A college with an overall student-teacher ratio of twenty to one can, in each semester, guarantee every student at least one very small class, two reasonably small classes, and one large class. Not only is this an acceptable, desirable mix of classroom situations, it also requires that roughly one in every four faculty members be capable of conducting a large lecture class.

We sometimes hear that the lecture method is an inferior form of instruction. Any experienced educator knows this cliché for what it is: an academic old wives' tale, presumably encouraged by those unable to hold an audience. Just as not every doctor should be allowed to perform surgery, not every professor should be allowed to use the lecture method. In the hands of a great lecturer, however, it can be one of the most effective means for the encouragement of learning, often awakening the interest of students more than either discussion or the written word would. A gifted lecturer brings the subject to life for hundreds of students, communicating his or her own commitment to what has been discovered and written, as well as conveying excitement about the ideas under discussion. Students are then eager to read works that otherwise would have been only dull requirements. We should also remember that the seminar is a widely abused institution, to which faculty and students often come totally unprepared; its minute scale is no guarantee of quality.

If a president intends to make a difference, he or she must master the financial details of the institution and not simply leave them to a financial vice-president. The preparation of the academic budget is the process by which the academic agenda of the university is determined. For instance, if resources are limited (as they almost always are), money allocated for a building is money unavailable for the recruitment of faculty. Excellent education can take place, of course, between first-rate teachers and first-rate students even if they meet in dull offices, teach and are taught in old-fashioned classrooms, and work in extremely modest physical facilities. Consequently, the improvement of the quality of faculty and students must clearly take precedence over allocation of funds for new or renovated facilities. Decisions about where money should be spent are decisions that profoundly influence an institution's academic programs and their quality.

An effective college president also functions as a member of the faculty. If intellectual achievements do not allow the president to hold his or her own in the university's intellectual "pecking order," he or she is at a great disadvantage. If his or her intellectual competence is manifest, however, he or she can ignore the ruling clichés and assert the capacity for judgment, not only in the appointment of faculty, deans, and departmental chairs, but also in the recruitment and selection of students. He or she also can take a hand in the development of the institution's curriculum. No college president who understands his or her role as educator will leave the curriculum solely in the hands of other faculty.

As an educator, as one among other faculty members on the campus, the college president must never pander to students. Instead, the president must serve as their mentor and teacher—frequently on moral issues, since he or she has scant opportunity to teach classroom subjects. The president may find that some fads are harmless and ignore them; on other occasions, he or she may find it necessary to resist the demands of students, denying them the luxury of self-righteousness. During the Vietnam War, the leadership of a number of college presidents was vitiated by their inability to distinguish criminal trespassing and gun-law violations from the rights of free speech and assembly. The integrity of their institutions was frequently undermined by their failure to ensure that people with all points of view—not just those of whom the more vociferous students and protestors approved—were allowed to speak on campus. Today, once again, shrill minorities sometimes threaten the freedom of speech of individuals invited to speak at universities; once again, prejudice and blind ideological commitment threaten the unbiased search for truth, which is so crucial to education.

It may be unfashionable to say so, but students are not teachers. No leader of a university worth his or her salt will tell students, "You can teach us as much as we can teach you." What parent would pay tens of thousands of dollars a year to send a child to an institution where the president, the dean, and the faculty were no better qualified to teach students than the students were to teach them? Faculty—who, on the average, have been working twenty years longer than their students to advance in knowledge and competence—should, with rare exceptions, be better qualified than their students.

College presidents who try to educate their students do not guarantee their own popularity, but they do preserve their institutions' educational missions. They ensure the independence of their colleges or universities from ideological fads and remain faithful to the Socratic pursuit of truth. No person, Socrates thought, is ever likely to attain the

18

truth; but educated men and women approach the truth with ever-closer approximation, providing a more and more likely account of reality.

A college president who seeks to be not just a manager but an educator is amply rewarded when he or she sees students beginning to value the difficult search for truth more than they value the simple ideological nostrums that flatter their vanity and disguise their ignorance. It is only through the difficult search for truth that students begin to discover their true selves. As Nietzsche says, in his essay "Schopenhauer as Educator,"

> Your true teachers, the men who formed you and educated you, revealed to you what is the true original sense and basic stuff of your nature. . . . And that is the secret of all education and culture; it does not give artificial limbs, wax noses, or corrective lenses—rather, that which can give those gifts is merely a caricature of education. Education, on the contrary, is liberation, the clearing of all weeds, rubble, and vermin that might harm delicate shoots, a radiance of light and warmth, a loving, falling rustle of rain by night.

The college president who is truly a leader understands that "education is liberation" and that his or her role is to clear away "all weeds, rubble, and vermin that might harm the delicate shoots." It is the president's task to help create the context in which the authentic individual, the civilized citizen, may emerge.

John Silber is president of Boston University.

*For the president in these dramatically changing times, myriad
issues always seem to have more urgency than education,
but nothing else is so important.*

Focusing on
Educational Issues

Robert H. McCabe

The student wrote: "This letter is one of the first I can write in English
and I would like to share with you my own satisfaction and to appreciate
the support we have received from Miami–Dade Community College in
our process of adjustment to this new society." This letter said so much
about why our college exists: to assist all who wish to try to improve
themselves, for their own benefit and that of our community. It reminded
me, as president, that my most important responsibility is to see that the
institution's commitment is fulfilled—in other words, to be the educational leader.

The role of president of an urban community college has changed
significantly during the twenty-five years that I have been a college administrator. Specifically, today the president's attention is being focused either
outside the institution or on operational concerns, and the result is that
educational issues are most often left to others.

When I first came to Miami–Dade in 1963, as assistant to the
president, there was great optimism about America. Industry was growing, there was substantial support for civil rights goals, and there was a
widely held belief that massive federal initiatives would quickly bring
minorities into the position of sharing equally in the good things this
nation has to offer. The hundreds of new community colleges that opened

J. L. Fisher and M. W. Tack (eds.). *Leaders on Leadership: The College Presidency.*
New Directions for Higher Education, no. 61. San Francisco: Jossey-Bass, Spring 1988.

in the early 1960s were a clear expression of that optimism. Funding was delivered routinely by state legislatures using full-time-equivalent (FTE) formulas; in Florida, there was even a funding recalculation if enrollment exceeded projections. In our case, the Florida Community College Division took care of legislative matters with so little local assistance that there were legislators from our district whom the college's president had never met. In a growth situation, the incremental cost for each added student is less than the base cost per student; thus, with FTE formulas, administrative errors disappeared in a rising tide of additional income. For college administrators, it was wonderful.

We were caught up in enthusiasm for the "community college movement"; throughout the country, among the staff, and in the community there was great pride in two-year colleges. There was a continuing need to develop additional programs and educational approaches to meet new challenges and opportunities. In this environment, there were very limited financial problems. Educational program development had an unavoidably high priority, and governmental and community issues were effectively handled by others. Community college presidents concentrated on internal matters, especially those concerning education. The literature of those times clearly indicates that those presidents were the educational leaders of their institutions.

The environment is very different in the late 1980s. There is less optimism about the future, especially among minorities. Public dissatisfaction with educational institutions is shown by lessened legislative support and by dramatically increased regulation and state bureaucracy. Tax revenues are not providing enough to fund all the important needs of society. Independent colleges and universities have begun to receive state funding, and, in response, community colleges have begun private fundraising. Court rulings and litigation have become a normal part of operations. Over the past decade, the failure of faculty salaries to keep pace with those in other professions has spawned aggressive faculty unions and organizations.

In these circumstances, the president is continually pulled away from educational issues by the urgency of other concerns. These are dominated by issues that others want to have addressed, many concerning state agencies and few concerning education. There is also a growing need for attention to budget issues as well as to organized faculty negotiation and other faculty issues. Building support among legislators, defending the institution from the negative effects of legislation, and dealing with bureaucracy, public relations, and fundraising are other concerns.

In the current environment, it is difficult but essential for a president to give primary attention to educational issues. The world and this nation are in a period of fundamental change, and community colleges must respond with educational improvements that are designed for the times and have the prospect of benefiting our society. We need to address the challenges and opportunities of the seemingly unbridgeable gap between the competence of our population and the skills required in the information age. We need to explore the promise of information technology to improve learning. We need to examine the utility of research on teaching and learning. We also need to consider the impending mass retirement of our aging faculty.

Each person interprets issues on the basis of experience and role. Clearly, the president is the only person in the college whose view is not constrained by role, and he or she must be the person who interprets the institution's mission and program in the context of current social needs. The community college president must be as expert in assessing social issues and as well versed in educational developments as the biology professor is in his or her discipline. By role, the president is the institution's public spokesperson and is looked to for leadership. He or she has the most power to shape the institution's direction and decisions. Most important, major program changes or improvements are likely when they are supported by the chief executive, and their prospects for success are greatest when the chief executive provides necessary leadership.

I lead an educational institution with a mission of great importance to our nation and community, and to which I am passionately committed. The institution is supported by the public because of the educational benefits it provides, and the rationale for the college's existence is its educational program. These are the reasons I am here and enjoy my role. Regardless of other requirements, my primary priority as a college president is that of providing educational leadership.

Robert H. McCabe is president of Miami–Dade Community College in Miami, Florida.

It is intimidating to preside over an institution so large as to be unknowable in terms of detail and personal familiarity and so complex as to be mysterious in most of the knowledge pursued and taught within it.

The University Presidency Today: A Word for the Incumbents

Steven Muller

Where are the great college presidents of today? Few of us who lead major universities have escaped this question, asked in a plaintive—and implicitly accusatory—tone. The question, in fact, is not merely rhetorical—it constitutes an indictment. The questioner has in mind the Gilmans, Eliots, Hutchins, or Conants of the past; he or she sees only those of us who currently hold office and finds us wanting. We seem pleasant enough, the questioner may suggest reassuringly, even able, diligent, and competent; but none of us is a great leader, none the present voice or conscience or inspiration of higher learning. We are perceived, our questioner will inform us with great courtesy, as lacking the aura, the eccentricity, the genius of greatness. We suffice rather than impress. We may stand tall, but we do not tower. We plod along in our loafers and fail to fill the giant footsteps of our predecessors. And—at least in my own experience—there is inevitably a ritual conclusion to this dialogue: "Well," says my interlocutor with just the right blend of pity and com-

Adapted from *Festschrift* in tribute to Dr. Arthur M. Sackler, and reprinted with permission from the *Johns Hopkins APL Technical Digest*, 1986, 7, 217–220.

J. L. Fisher and M. W. Tack (eds.). *Leaders on Leadership: The College Presidency.*
New Directions for Higher Education, no. 61. San Francisco: Jossey-Bass, Spring 1988.

fort, "you must spend all your time raising money so that you cannot do much else—and you do raise a lot of money."

Having now heard this with some frequency over the years, I have become more accepting both of my own inadequacies as well as those of my peers. Yet the question rankles. Where are the great college presidents of today? How inferior, compared to our legendary forebears, are those of us who occupy the presidencies of major universities? If it is true that none among us has attained the dominant stature, the mantle of national advocacy that is expected of at least one or some of us, why is this so. My answer—biased and self-serving as any response from someone in my position obviously has to be—is that we university presidents of today may very well be inferior to our predecessors but that what we do, how we do it, and how we are perceived are so very different from their circumstances that their comparative superiority is not wholly self-evident. I do not challenge their greatness. I do not assert ours. Instead, I submit merely that the finest of our predecessors rose to an opportunity that may no longer exist for those of us who hold university presidencies today. At the risk of arguing only that we are mutants rather than pygmies, let me try to make my case.

The case consists mainly of a single point: The major research university of today is a radically different institution than its predecessor of three or four decades ago. The most obvious difference is size. As recently as the 1940s and even early 1950s, a university was not very much larger than a college. The question as to where the great college presidents of the present day are to be found assumes, in fact, that this is still the case. I speak, however, only of the presidencies of major research universities, and those institutions now are hugely different from colleges. Where once a university was a collegiate institution that granted the doctorate and harbored professional as well as undergraduate schools, there have now evolved in the United States between fifty and one hundred major research universities that are megasize—numbering their students in tens of thousands, their faculties and administrative cadres in thousands, their buildings and their acreage in hundreds. True, colleges also are larger today than they used to be; but today's major research university differs as much from a college as an aircraft carrier from a frigate. And, to stay with the image, today's university has evolved from its own past as much as today's nuclear-powered behemoth aircraft carrier is a different vessel from the early flattops.

Much could now be said about the difference produced by size alone, but let me offer just a few observations about the impact of sheer size on the university presidency. To begin with, the president as a person is far less evident than before. He or she cannot possibly know personally, nor be personally known by, the thousands upon thousands who compose the university community each year. The president may be visible to all, at one time or another; he or she may work hard to know many. But to most, the president remains an office rather than a person, a symbol more than a reality. Furthermore, although the president may still make the ultimate judgment on major decisions, sheer institutional size tends also to diminish personal presidential authority. To most of the people in the university, the decisions of greatest interest and relevance need to be made and are made at a level much closer to them than the apex of the central administration. The need to see the president, even directly to involve the office of the president, is relatively rare. And few decisions come to the president, or should come to him or her *de novo*. Staff effort—staff involvement—normally precedes presidential consideration or is called on at once to augment presidential initiative. The personality of the office still counts—so do the style and the articulation—but the size of the enterprise imposes the restraints of process. Perhaps the simplest effect of size on the presidency—and the greatest—is so obvious as to escape attention: It is the sheer volume of work required just to keep up with all the facets of so large an institution. The quantity of problems to be solved does, in fact, increase in direct proportion to the number of people involved. No president can be aware of everything that happens in the university, but no president can afford long to be in ignorance of most that happens; the result is endless presidental hours devoted to the effort of keeping track of the enormity of scope encompassed by the major research university.

Not size alone, however, sharply differentiates the university today from what it was but twoscore years ago. Complexity plays a competing role with size. The very research intensity that justifies "research university" as a descriptive name subjects the institution to the ultimate in the fragmentation of human knowledge. Because it attracts and fosters the most advanced and specialized talents among its professors and students, the research university offers a kaleidoscope of intricate inquiries that represents not coherence but the glitter and sparkle of a myriad of precious fragments that often seem to bear little relationship one to another. Much could be said on this subject as well; but for the university president, it presents the challenge of continually trying to learn what is happening to the very substance of the research and teaching enterprise. I have myself described my presidency in part as a never-ending seminar. One is blessed with the best of teachers; in my experience, no professor, even a Nobel Laureate, has ever failed when asked to make the effort to enlighten the university president as to the nature and significance of his or her research. But as one moves from lasers to restriction enzymes, from very large system integration to magnetic resonance imaging, from gender studies in East Asia to structuralism, from the nondestructive evaluation of materials to the impact of the space telescope on astrophysics, one may aspire at best to fatigued acquaintance with a great many wonders but never to confident or easy comprehension. Yet one must keep on trying—and across the board—even while discovery and innovation multiply faster than rabbits. How can one recruit some, while encouraging others to stay or leave, or authorize new laboratories or bless the creation of new departments, without at least a rudimentary sense of the work actually being done? When faculty achievements bring public acclaim, how could the president of the institution maintain a pose of blissful ignorance? And even more directly to the point, one wonders whether those who speak so fluently of fundraising have ever thought that the person who asks for support must know not only whom to ask but also what to ask for and why a particular project is of importance and priority. Hours of hard learning in a bewildering array of unfamiliar subjects go into even elementary awareness of what merits support and why.

It is intimidating to preside over an institution so large as to be unknowable in terms of detail and personal familiarity and so complex as to be mysterious in most of the knowledge pursued and taught within it. A good-sized ego is required to cope with such intimidation; that I do possess and seem to find among my peers as well. But is there an ego large enough today to allow me or any of my peers to claim that we understand it all and speak for the whole enterprise of the major research university as if from Olympus? Even forty years ago, our predecessors could still either believe or cherish the illusion that they understood at least the major facets of what was being done in their universities. Today this may not be altogether impossible for the president of an undergraduate college. It is no longer possible for the president of a major research university. My peers and I may not be naturally humble, but we may not be presumed to be actually stupid. Absent stupidity, we may be more sharply aware of the extent of our ignorance than were our predecessors, mostly because the limits of our knowledge are daily stretched, in anguish. And that may play a role in holding us back from grasping the mantle of national leadership even in our own domain of higher learning.

Sometimes it is said of us as university presidents that we have become merely managers. There is, I think, some truth in that, although the "merely" gives me pause. As chief executive officers of our institutions, we are, of course, expected to manage. There are all those people, in their thousands; all those buildings; all that research; and all that money. Our annual budgets are counted in the hundreds of millions of dollars. As presidents, we are apt to be nominal landlords to students who may number in the thousands and, in some cases, also to faculty and staff. We have responsibility as well for extracurricular activities—a multimillion dollar industry for most of my colleagues if, happily, not for me. And there are other managerial obligations: While I do not dispose of a small airline, as some of my peers do, I am responsible for a hotel, as many of them are; and I am ultimately responsible for the disposal of radioactive waste (from radiation treatment for cancer), the operation of a nonhuman primate breeding facility, the maintenance of a small fleet of research vessels, and campuses overseas. There are the university press and the academic support services, especially the university library system. There is some responsibility for the teaching hospital—hospitals in the plural in my case—as well as prepaid health plans and HMOs (health maintenance organizations). There is policy for and supervision of thousands of nonacademic personnel—nearly 5,000, in my case—without whom the institution would cease to function, just as surely as if all the faculty left or no students enrolled. So, yes, we are managers and—also, yes—we are expected to raise money as well. Our revered predecessors were, of course, managers as well. But there can be no doubt that the size, complexity, and diversity of the major research university place vastly greater managerial responsibilities in the hands of those of us who serve as president today than was true three or four decades ago.

Let me assume at this point that I have stated my case that there is a radical difference between the job of a major research university president now and in the earlier days of our great predecessors. By way of further reflection as to why none of us now in office has attained greater national stature, I have some thoughts to offer that involve circumstances in the world outside our institutions. One might by now assume that the demands of our assignment are so great that my peers and I have no time left for any other activity at all. However, this is not the case. We do quite a lot away from our campuses—in fact, probably more than we should; but most of it represents what I would like to refer to as distraction. We serve on boards and panels in the field of education; we testify before legislatures and other public bodies; we give speeches before a variety of public and academic audiences; we travel abroad to meet with our peers overseas and to become familiar with some of their universities; we meet with our alumni in major cities across the country, and even abroad; we call on foundations and other donors. Our predecessors did all these things also but not to the same extent. The problem today is that travel is so quick and—at least apparently—simple that we tend to agree to do too much, on an overly compressed schedule. One-day journeys from one coast to the other are stock in trade. Three- or four-day journeys to Europe are not infrequent. I am surely not unique among my peers with an alumni trip that took me to eight cities in five days. This kind of mobility is useful: It widens our perspective; it provides some public exposure and the occasional opportunity for public advocacy; and it affords relief from the heavy day-to-day office schedule. It is, however, a major distraction as well—last-minute overloads before a trip and awful accumulations afterward, reports and papers read in haste on airplanes, fatigue produced by overcrowded schedules, and the tension of delays that frustrate tight and orderly planning.

All I mean to say here is our pace is faster than that of our predecessors, and our geographic range is greater. And this, of course, is true not only of university presidents but of virtually all American professionals. It may well follow, then, that we are less serene than our predecessors; and I believe this indeed to be the case. It does not obviously follow, however, that we are less reflective; and I do not believe that this is necessarily so. Is what we say always so dull, so trivial, so insignificant that we attract little attention even though we are heard in public with some frequency? Maybe so—certainly so, all too often, in my own case. But to me it seems that there is another set of circumstances involved as well. Earlier I spoke of great former university presidents in terms of dominant stature, of national advocacy; I did so because that is the frame of reference in which the original question is asked. If greatness is equated with national stature, then part of the problem with today's university presidents may be that we are not media personalities.

In a society whose attention span has shrunk from earlier times and that reads less and less, national recognition derives primarily from national television and secondarily from newspapers and weeklies. On the one hand, the thoughtful—and lengthy—address, the colorful anecdote, and the detailed exposition of the complicated have been largely replaced by brief remarks, one-liners, and headlines or captions. On the other hand, prolonged and repeated national television exposure has elevated to national stature (greatness?) not only politicians but also television commentators, articulate athletes, and other entertainers. University presidents do not make news very often; and when they do, the news is often bad. We are not—most of us—showbiz. We do not star in our own commercials because our universities do not use commercials, at least not yet. But I do not doubt that if one of us were to narrate a popular weekly television program—perhaps on science or health—then a new star might be born and one of us might have, at last, the national stature of a Carl Sagan or of a Dr. Ruth. We may well be at fault in not attempting to use "the media"—television in particular—to greater advantage. The only point I wish to make here is that the path to national stature in our times is radically different from the one that was open to our predecessors.

But, having said all of the above, I have a still different and, to me, more satisfying answer to the question of why there are no great university presidents today. There may not be, is my answer; but there are still great universities. In fact, where there were perhaps a score of great universities four decades ago, there are now three or four times as many. The quality and scope of university research today make the research effort of forty years ago look tiny in comparison. And someone does preside over each of these great major research universities. There was a time—in the 1960s and early 1970s—when the pressures of Vietnam and student unrest reduced presidential incumbencies to the point where many of our immediate predecessors held office for only a few years. Today, however, a goodly number of my peers and I have been in office for more than a decade and hope to serve somewhat longer still. We are charged to make decisions; and over the years we have made many, not all of them good or right. We have had a hand in great changes: new programs begun and older ones reduced, eliminated, or merged. We may be blessed with an end to the drastic growth in numbers of students and matching numbers of faculty and staff, but we may be cursed with stark reductions in support. We are presiding, still, over the transition of our institutions into an era of new communication—of knowledge stored, recalled, displayed, and manipulated in staggering quantity and with dazzling speed. Our scholars and graduates soar the heavens in rockets, plumb the depths of the seas, examine the microcosmics of animate and inanimate matter, and probe the workings of the human brain and mind. Our pride is in the institutions that we serve and that, in turn, serve society—and serve well.

And, yes, we have our dreams of greatness—not for ourselves, but for our universities. We are—each of us—builders. Our task is to help to remodel our institutions for tomorrow—for the students who come anew each year, for scholars who will acquire knowledge that as yet eludes us, for discoveries and techniques that will enhance the human condition anew. Let us admit it: We are not great ourselves. But we serve great institutions with a great purpose, and that is no mean task. We lack the dash and daring of a single skipper at the helm; instead, we pace the automated captain's bridge of an ocean liner. But as we leave and enter port each academic year, there is still pleasure and satisfaction in the job done, and to be done again. No, there may be no great university presidents today. But there are great universities, greater than yesterday's. And the men and women who captain them are no unworthy breed.

Steven Muller is president of The Johns Hopkins University.

Effective college presidents do not preside; they lead, energized by a vision and guided by an agenda.

Some Good Advice

George A. Pruitt

Until recently, there has not been much available to guide those in our profession aspiring to the contemporary college and university presidency. Therefore, the most useful tool available for my preparation to be a chief executive officer was the good advice of others who had gone before me. Not surprisingly, most of the discussions I have about the nature of presidential leadership are with faculty, graduate students, and colleagues wanting insight into the office as they attempt to acquaint themselves with one of the most challenging leadership positions our society has to offer. So it is, therefore, with a sense of doing for others what was done for me that I offer what I hope will be good advice for those who choose a path similar to mine.

1. *Do not seek the presidency unless you want to be the president.* It is a position that makes extraordinary demands upon your family, your privacy, your time, your talent, and your physical energy. Be prepared to commit all of these things. As Ness (1971) observed, "The successful presidents and deans I have known were in administration because they wanted to be in it and stayed because they had some sort of masochistic love for it. . . . I believe their success lies partially in the fact that they have adopted a kind of humanistic approach, seeing administration as a scholarly discipline with an inherent integrity and value" (p. 5).

2. *Do not want to be the president unless you do so for appropriate reasons.* If your ambition is grounded in a quest for status, visibility,

J. L. Fisher and M. W. Tack (eds.). *Leaders on Leadership: The College Presidency.*
New Directions for Higher Education, no. 61. San Francisco: Jossey-Bass, Spring 1988.

influence, or prestige, then you misunderstand the nature of the office, for these are hollow things, incapable of sustaining themselves and of no intrinsic value as objectives or ends. On the other hand, if your aspirations are motivated by a vision or an agenda, then the presidency is the principal platform and pulpit from which to influence collective purposes toward a noble end.

All the effective presidential leaders I have known and admired have had visions for their institutions that went far beyond current conditions. They have had in common a sense of creation—a clear view of what the institutions ought to have been but were not. When I first came to Edison, in December of 1982, I visited the Princeton University president, William Bowen. I had been at Edison several months. He had been at Princeton over fifteen years, but I recall his clear sense of how Princeton could be better and the way his energies were directed at making it so.

Colleges and universities are dynamic living institutions. They go forward or they atrophy, but they never stand still. Few institutions in our society depend more on the consensus of their members to achieve collective purposes. Building such consensus into a set of organizing principles that are well understood and enthusiastically supported is the challenge of the presidency. As Marvel (1974) has advised, marshal the talents of your community "to advance institutional goals; become the functional leader or the status leadership will be hollow in effect and satisfaction; maintain good health, pray and have good luck" (p. 73). The effective presidents I know are infectious in their spirit, enthusiasm, and passion for their institutions' missions. Much has been written about the frustrations and pitfalls of the office, but no one would trade them for the gratifications received from a college serving its public well. Effective college presidents do not preside; they lead, energized by a vision and guided by an agenda. When the vision is gone and the agenda completed, the effectiveness of the president has ended.

3. *Find the very best people you can and help them to be successful.* Recruit and reward bright, hardworking, enthusiastic professionals who share the values of the college and a commitment to the purpose of the institution. Delegate enough authority for them to achieve the tasks for which they are responsible. Find out how you can help them to be successful, hold them accountable for their actions, and reward them for their achievements. In their success, the institution and your presidency will be successful. Strive to be open in your communications, be candid in your evaluations, and encourage good people to be adventurous and to take risks. Challenge them to do good things, and create an organization that becomes an incubator for the achievement of others. Great institutions are great only because they have good people who do great things around a common purpose.

4. *Be consistent, be predictable, and be decisive.* As President Eisen-

hower once pointed out, most presidential decisions are difficult; the easy ones are made in other places. There is, in my view, a difference between the right decision and the correct decision. The right decision reveals itself only after the fact, when the scenario has played itself out and one has the benefit of hindsight. The correct decision is the best decision that can be made in a timely manner with the information currently available. Of course, you always hope that the correct decision turns out to be the right decision; but in either event, you must decide. Issues that come into your office fuzzy and depicted in various shades of gray must leave clearly defined and intelligently articulated. The deliberative nature of scholarly debate is important and worthwhile in the culture of the academy, but the same deliberation will devastate and gridlock your decision making. Problems may not be solved, but they must be resolved. Choices must be made between legitimately competing points of view, and one must be prepared to stand accountable for and be comfortable with the consequences of those choices. For the president, in most cases, even the wrong decision, well made, is better than no decision at all.

5. *Prepare yourself experientially.* Spend time understanding the nature and demands of the office, and try to gain experience in areas where you will be called on to perform. The president is the leader of an academic enterprise, but he or she is also the chief executive of a multi-million-dollar, complex organization. As the principal manager, you are responsible for issues related to finance, physical plant, energy conservation, complex legal questions, labor relations, purchasing, philanthropy, and a complicated regulatory environment. One hopes to have the deftness of touch by which red tape and bureaucracy become systems of achieving educational and management objectives; or, as former President Wells of Indiana University wrote, the president must "be born with the physical strength of a Greek athlete, the cunning of a Machiavelli, the wisdom of a Solomon, the courage of a lion, if possible. But in any case he must be born with the stomach of a goat" (Bennis, 1973, p. 17).

I offer for your benefit some good advice given to me by my uncle: "If you want to really learn how to do something, find a master and learn from him." I have been extraordinarily lucky in my life to have known several masters of this art, and I have benefited enormously from their mentoring. To the extent that I have achieved, it has been as a consequence of the work and lessons learned from others.

6. *Choose an environment with which you are compatible.* Colleges and their trustees select the president, but the president must also select the college and the trustees. Our institutions are enormously diverse in their patterns of governance, both externally and internally. In addition, each college or university has developed a culture and complex protocols in which the president must operate. In the public sector, the president is

expected to provide leadership in a variety of structural and political contexts. The president, the board, the college, and the controlling external environment must have a common understanding about the nature and scope of presidential leadership. It is relatively easy for the college's constituents and the new president to agree on the proper mission and direction of the institution; the difficulty is determining the division of authority and accountability in achieving these various purposes.

There are different points of view on the various spheres of authority and prerogatives in an institution, but the authority and responsibility of the president, with respect to trustees and other campus constituencies, must not be ambiguous. Leadership philosophy, management style, and division of labor between the president and the controlling spheres of influence must be compatible. Dissonance on these matters invites unfortunate consequences.

7. *Do not get seduced by the office.* The contemporary college presidency is an important and visible leadership position in a very important institution. The office of the president is the personification and embodiment of the institution. The respect and deference accorded to the president are given to the office, to the college, and, to a lesser degree, to the individual. Wherever you go, you are the president seven days a week, twenty-four hours a day. You will confer with the powerful and the prestigious. Your opinion will be sought on the great issues of the day. While you must take your responsibility to this office very, very seriously, you can never take yourself very seriously. You are a symbol of the collective achievements, history, and aspirations of an extraordinary set of people. Always be protective of the dignity, symbols, and prerogatives of your office, but never confuse the regency of your office with the person of its incumbent.

8. *Know when to leave.* I have been an observer of the American college presidency for over twenty years and a practitioner for five. It takes no special insight to recognize that the college presidency can be a volatile office. It is also well known that the burdens of leadership can become exceedingly heavy over time. There is no such thing as a standard presidential tenure. The tenure of one's presidency should coincide with its effectiveness, but this idea is often difficult for the incumbent to perceive. Clearly, presidential leadership must enjoy the confidence of trustees and of important campus constituencies, but the vitality and currency of the presidential agenda are just as important. When the president has done all he or she knows how to do, when the institution has come as far as the incumbent can move it, or when new faces resurrect old issues, then the president and those close to the office must prepare for new leadership. Whether this occurs in five years or twenty-five years is a function of the energies of the individual and the nature of the campus community (unless, of course, you are President Hesburgh of Notre

Dame, whose vigorous leadership never atrophied even after thirty-five years). It has been my misfortune to witness colleagues with great presidencies end ignobly because they stayed too long; I have seen some presidencies, which should have concluded in celebration, end in controversy because of timing.

9. *Finally, enjoy yourself.* If you are as lucky as I, you will have a board of trustees that is competent, supportive, independent, attentive, yet unintrusive; professional colleagues who are competent, stimulating, pleasant, and committed to our common purpose; and the greatest students in the nation. My institution benefits from our extraordinary singleness of purpose: We exist to serve adult learners. Our students, whose average age is forty, are not only thirsty for learning but grateful for the opportunities we provide. Naturally, I hope I am smart enough to take my own advice and recognize when it is time to leave—but for now, my plate is full, I revel in the work we do, the agenda is not yet completed, and I am having a ball.

References

Bennis, W. *The Leaning Ivory Tower.* San Francisco: Jossey-Bass, 1973.

Marvel, J. A. Comment included on the survey instrument. In G. A. Pruitt, "Blueprint for Leadership: The American College Presidency." Unpublished doctoral dissertation, The Union Graduate School, 1974.

Ness, F. W. *An Uncertain Glory.* San Francisco: Jossey-Bass, 1971.

George A. Pruitt is president of Thomas A. Edison State College, New Jersey's college for adults, in Trenton.

Good leadership depends on the ability to tolerate anxiety,
loneliness, and the threat of unpopularity. This ability is more
likely to be developed by the observation of good role models
in action than through formal training.

The Apprenticeship
Approach to Leadership

Stephen J. Trachtenberg

Leadership is a subject often discussed these days. In preparing to address
it, I asked myself some difficult questions. Can leadership in fact be
taught? Is it an activity that, even in an academic setting, lends itself to
an instructional as opposed to an apprenticeship approach? Can we do
very much to prepare effective university presidents, beyond seeing that
their preparatory years are spent working with and reporting to effective
senior administrators inside or outside the academic world? Rather to my
own surprise, I came up with a personal vote in favor of apprenticeship,
based on several considerations.

   1. *Effective leadership is less a matter of skills, talents, or even polit-*
ical savvy than of the ability to tolerate very high levels of anxiety and
loneliness. A lot of what is being written or said on leadership these days
is based on the fact that our world, at many different levels, seems to
have an actual hunger for leadership. This hunger, in turn, is probably
connected to the fact that our designated leaders are experiencing unprece-
dented levels of criticism and muckraking from media that are carefully
attuned to what the public actually wants to see, hear, and read.

   Nevertheless, leaders are actual people who are needed to run
actual academic institutions. Our concern is less with media images than
with the day-to-day realities in need of effective management. This per-

J. L. Fisher and M. W. Tack (eds.). *Leaders on Leadership: The College Presidency.*
New Directions for Higher Education, no. 61. San Francisco: Jossey-Bass, Spring 1988.

spective has caused me to conclude that good leadership depends on the ability to tolerate anxiety, loneliness, and the threat of unpopularity, an ability more likely to come from observing good role models than from undergoing formal training.

We often rather casually refer to the "top of the pyramid." What few of us bother to notice, however, is that the apex of that particular geometric form can also be envisioned as the end of a bowling alley or the target on a shooting range—especially if we imagine a dozen bowling balls or bullets arriving simultaneously. In other words, the pyramid is a form in which demands, needs, complaints, bright ideas, protests, suggestions, conflicts, and other high-pressure forms of ideation flow upward until they reach the point at which "the buck stops."

It is difficult for those who have not experienced it to imagine the pressure often brought to bear on a university president when a decision of even moderate significance needs to be made. Because universities are, in a certain sense, public trusts, the telephone rings and the in-box overflows with urgings from constituencies like administrators and faculty at other institutions, elected officials, spouses and children of those concerned, trustees and donors, and Nobel Prize winners. The authors of all these communications fall into three primary categories: those who are for, those who are against, and, usually, a large number who can be classified as "other."

Only one thing is certain: Whatever decision gets made will be wrong for some vociferous and even powerful people. No wonder the men and women who serve as leaders in academic institutions sometimes succumb to paralyzing *angst*, to "going with the flow," or to bribing the opposed constituencies with a series of self-contradictory decisions aimed to pacify. No wonder the nominal leader sometimes looks like a very frightened rabbit whose mind is totally focused on survival, rather than on making sound decisions. With muckraking so pervasive these days, no wonder academic leaders run scared of local and regional newspapers, as well as of the *Chronicle of Higher Education*.

2. *Role models are particularly important, because today's leaders must cope with a decline in manners and in self-restraint, which it is libelous to call barbarian.* As historians have long understood, the so-called barbarians who invaded the Roman Empire were mainly concerned with adapting and assimilating it. The titles they assumed and the coins they minted reflected their intimate knowledge and awe of the system they were so relentlessly infiltrating. Even Attila was moved by the pleas of an unarmed Pope to spare the city of Rome from attack.

In contrast, today's leaders especially in academic life, often confront a range of behaviors intended to influence their decisions. These behaviors range from journalistic attack and public libel to picketing, shouting, sit-ins, and outright violence. It is no longer front-page news when a speaker, invited to air his or her views as part of the competition between ideas that is the *raison d' être* of a university, is howled down before uttering a word. This pervasive deterioration in academic discourse and advocacy affects the university president even more strongly, because he or she sees it daily. Because this new counterethic of "no rules whatsoever" is so open ended, it can even raise the leader's anxiety about personal physical safety and possible threats aimed at family and friends.

During my pilgrimage toward the university presidency I now hold, I had the privilege of working with a number of leaders who were able to cope with threats that sometimes had physical overtones. My blood ran a little colder, and so, I assume, did theirs; but they stuck to their convictions because they believed the right action had to take precedence over personal anxiety. Once, when the threat was political rather than physical, I watched a member of Lyndon Johnson's cabinet say no to Lyndon Johnson. That encouraged me, as an academic vice-president, to say no (on occasion) to my own boss. Thus, I was prepared to serve as a leader for whom the word *no* would not strike a chord of absolute terror when sent out to others or when sent back to me. Indeed, my apprenticeship and my role models served me well.

3. *Role models are vital to leaders who, today as always, need to cope with what is rather euphemistically termed "group dynamics."* In the social and behavioral sciences, rational models of the leader-led relationship have increasingly given way to scenarios in which initial idealization of a leader seems inexorably to give way to the desire to scapegoat him or her. This situation, in turn, leads either to the leader's termination or to a revival that amounts to a reidealization. The effective leader is increasingly envisioned as a responsive, quick-moving manipulator who relies on a good deal of intuition to thread his or her way through all the conflicts, coalitions, interest groups, and mutually hostile idealisms that need to be handled on an average day.

The need to cope with group dynamics makes it mandatory for the successful leader to develop a high degree of empathy—the ability to understand another person's point of view "from the inside" in order to influence those who are seeking to influence him or her. The ability to empathize in this way is probably inborn, although it can be sharpened over time. Certainly, ego-based needs must be moved to the back burner while the other person's ego becomes the focus.

Since leaders have to deal with dozens of people simultaneously, this aspect of the leadership role can be described as one of improvisatory orchestration. It requires a very high degree of stamina and persistence, the ability to move rapidly and widely without succumbing to vertigo, and the ability to entertain a variety of hypotheses, scenarios, and other possibilities without feeling as if one's brain were being pulled apart by wild horses. Once again, these are abilities best developed through observing, from the inside, the daily behaviors of an established and successful leader.

Having said all these things about the virtues of apprenticeship versus a pedagogical approach to leadership training, I may appear to have painted myself into a corner. This is a sourcebook, after all, heavily oriented toward academic life, which in turn is deeply involved with pedagogy. Moreover, an apprenticeship system is unlikely to be successful in turning out the numbers of effective leaders required in either the academic context or the corporate and governmental sectors. Is there not anything we can do, therefore, other than return to the training norms of a medieval guild?

Where the presidencies of long-lived colleges or universities are concerned, I wonder whether anything but an apprenticeship system has ever truly existed in the United States. As we know, a vacancy of this kind draws a huge volume of applications and nominations; each of the potential presidents being brought to the school's attention is, it goes without saying, hyperbolically qualified in terms of education, accomplishment, personality, and so forth. What then ensues is an evaluation phase, in which the curricula vitae of those on the short list are probed, weighed, tested, assessed, and reassessed with an emphasis on the realities that underlie them. The comments likely to carry the most weight in this process are those of respected figures to whom the candidates reported for significant lengths of time, and who were not on the candidates' own lists of references. When an on-site visit is made to a candidate's current place of employment, observations by his or her present or former subordinates are likely to be evaluated carefully, with mere griping separated from shrewd observations based on long exposure. In short, the testing that takes place as the sheep are separated from the goats has a hands-on flavor that counterbalances the paper world of applications, vitae, and letters of reference. The theoretical leader is really being seen as an apprentice who may or may not have gained the abilities of a master.

How do we train and encourage strong leaders? A first step might be to convince potential leaders that they do not have to stand at the very peak of Mount Everest to maintain their self-respect. The news media deluge us with so many messianic pretensions that images of supreme potency become engraved on our minds: presidents, prime ministers, religious leaders, masterminds of corporate acquisition, Svengalis of marketing, and rock stars whose followers around the globe amount to a significant percentage of the human race. That is a truly heady brew, and its ability to intoxicate lies in the fact that leadership figures are always being defrocked or dethroned and replaced. The media universe is always brand new, yet it always implies that those currently featured on the front pages of *Time* and *Newsweek* will still be there for us as the years go by—that their positions are eternal.

That way madness lies. What we need in a curriculum for leadership is something that begins as early as the age of five or six: an educational process that teaches the young and the not-so-young to recognize the difference between their own very real selves and the hallucinations pouring in through the print and electronic media. Holding on to oneself is a goal very appropriate for those living in the modern world. It is also the only basis for becoming an effective leader.

Stephen J. Trachtenberg, president of the University of Hartford since 1977 and professor of law and public administration, will assume the presidency of the George Washington University in August 1988.

Allow the faculty to run the classrooms, the deans to run the year, and the vice-presidents to worry about next year. It is the president's job to be concerned about and provide for the future.

Interiors of the Presidency

Keith G. Briscoe

Civilization is a stream and banks. The stream is sometimes filled with blood from people killing, stealing, shouting, and doing things historians usually record, while on the banks, unnoticed, people build homes, make love, raise children, sing songs, write poetry.
The story of civilization is the story of what happened on the banks. Historians are pessimists because they ignore the banks for the river.

Will Durant

Although I have read Drucker, Peters and Waterman, Steiner and Dyer, and, of course, Odiorne, I confess that my style of leadership does not rely solely on these people or on MBO, PERT, or Theory Z. I guess that admission makes me either an eclectic or an eccentric.

Leadership is more than a vision, but no leadership style will work without a vision. A vision is a personal matter; it relies on point of view. Candidly sharing the source of one's ken is risky, because the process of recreating allows for little organization and no systematic flow. Still we have already established that I may be an eccentric, and so I invite you to walk down my path. See if you can hear what I feel.

A college: What is this challenging, consuming environment? Why does it hurt so? Where do I belong? Is anything my own? Is everything

J. L. Fisher and M. W. Tack (eds.). *Leaders on Leadership: The College Presidency.*
New Directions for Higher Education, no. 61. San Francisco: Jossey-Bass, Spring 1988.

part of everything? Do I belong to everyone? Does nothing belong to me? Where is ownership? Cannot anything be simple? Why does it take so long to get anything done? Why is everyone so hurried, rushed, and near burnout?

Problems: Oh, how we love them. Let us create one, borrow one, or worry that we may not be professional if we do not have one.

A college is a place driven by untold taskmasters, each demanding an elusive excellence, undefined and unyielding. Its description is elusive, but the learned high-court judges independently profess that they will know it when they see it. On my better days, is everyone blind?

From my perspective, a college is also a place to learn, to grow. It is a place to belong, to become. It is a place to seek that elusive excellence. Certainly, a college is not the lengthened shadow of one man or woman. It is the collective light of many people, all committed to the welfare of the whole.

At Buena Vista College, my role has been to find and know the soul of this college and to keep it always alert, always in mind. Because this is a college—a place of learning, a place of change—management style must reflect the environment: the vitality, the openness, and the flexibility of the classroom, of the library, between professors and students, and among the students themselves.

At a college, leadership is governed by one solitary, solid concept: We seek here to develop and cultivate the individual. To do that, we must give these individuals, our students, a chance at every imaginable idea. We must make them open to the disharmony, the cacophony of learning, for learning is not always harmonious; learning is conservatives having it out with liberals, behaviorists with Jungians, modernists with postmodernists. This flux, this chaos of ideas, must be encouraged. To seek harmony at a college is to stop learning. Leadership must acknowledge the flux: the irregularities, the anomalies of each part of the college community as they jostle, elbow, and clamor for attention. Leadership is to accept and encourage the chaos of each one doing his or her own thing. Know the price, and remember: Truth, honor, and honesty are the goals.

When the uniquely academic spirit is working, it gives back to you in ways you never imagined. Being part of your own world of ideas is demanding. Sharing ideas with others while shepherding your own is exhilarating. Sometimes you are admired for presenting a new idea; sometimes you let go of it. You watch it change and become clouded, recharged, even lost. There is no possession, no pride of ownership. Thrown into the collective, ideas breed ideas—more developed and evolved with each generation. Meanwhile, new powers of concentration are discovered; divergent views stimulate. This is living in a hothouse of intellectual thought. In all this confusion is freedom of ideas, fresh air blown in new directions you never knew existed. Working together, we are greater than we could ever be alone. We are carried to new heights. From chaos comes new order, decisions, and progress.

An institution that grows as rapidly as Buena Vista College—in academics, in facilities and equipment, and in endowment—develops a momentum. With momentum, new victories and visions are easily attracted, as well as more easily attained. A college needs milestones; it also needs celebration.

The fact is that we seldom stop to smell the roses; they are taken for granted. Celebrations are forgotten, lacking, or overlooked. That is sad, for we need touchstones. We study the milestones of history, but we do not take time to erect our own. We need them. We need stars—pilot stars. We must reward them, because from these stars come light that can be used by others for the self-directed journey of inquiry. We must be alert for pilot flags, raised by drifting faculty or lost students and signaling the need for leadership. Our pilot stars must share their navigational charts of moral and scientific codes with novice sailors; one cannot exist without the other.

The key is having a cohesive, knowledgeable, and dedicated staff. When you put the best minds to good use, you get the best of those minds. Time in hallways, classrooms, and offices for visiting, chatting, and listening is well spent. Elicit the wisdom of one staff member, and toss it into the arena for the next staff member. It is all right to encourage faculty to use the power that administrators frequently try to usurp. Give it back and let them run. Allow the faculty to run the classroom, the deans to run the year, and the vice-presidents to worry about next year. It is the president's job to be concerned about and provide for the future.

To believe in a long-term vision, to shape it, and to watch it become reality are rare and miraculous privileges. To be on the cutting edge is knowing where that edge is—for your school and for yourself; it is not being in the forefront of higher education, being the first experimental college, having the first value-added curriculum, or being the college with the fewest or the most course requirements. It means learning from the best of higher education and continuing to refine and simplify those ideas. To be on the cutting edge of education is both to know an idea is not marketable and not to care. It is to use both lateral and perpendicular thinking, without differentiating between them. The cutting edge means intellectual gymnastics, the very process of learning.

What makes a college a college? It is a noninstitution: a collective of people, a spirit, and a community. This collective—going in all its many conflicting, diverse directions—has to be encouraged and nurtured, as well as protected. There is a proper time for a president to feel resentment, anger, and passion because it is solely the president's duty to eliminate people who try to stop this unabashed community of learners.

In short, I love a college; and, as a college president, I have two types of responsibility. My daily responsibility is the preservation of all the things that make the faculty the most respected people on earth (by those who seek the truth) and the most feared (by those who seek the domination of others). My long-term responsibility is to hire correctly and provide the environment for a vision that includes the future of society. The role of this college is to help advance the society. Finally, I must further endow the college so that it need not depend on trends, short-term gains, or slogans for financial survival. It will not be my leadership, but the institution's, that will affect the vision of our changing society.

Keith G. Briscoe is president of Buena Vista College, Storm Lake, Iowa.

A president who has not stood alone against the bureaucracy and overruled it—in favor of a single student, a faculty member, or an unpopular issue—is not doing the job that needs to be done.

Taking the Risk and Making a Difference

Stephen Horn

The importance of character—moral and ethical integrity—to the American presidency is obvious, but the importance of strong character to the American college presidency is often overlooked. Still, nothing is more vital to institutional advancement. Unlike their predecessors in the nineteenth century, most presidents no longer teach required courses on moral philosophy to all graduating seniors. Nevertheless, contemporary university presidents can and should set set high ethical standards in the attitudes they express and the decisions they make.

One principal reason why character is crucial to institutional progress is that at the time of a president's selection, many issues are still parts of the unfolding future, which no one can accurately foresee. With respect to these issues, the character and the commitment to quality of the person selected are essential. Character in the college president is the consistent adherence to doing what is right and in the best long-term interest of the university, even at the price of one's popularity or one's job.

In all too many modern public universities, presidents find limited resources and indifference among faculty, students, staff, the community, and alumni. Unfortunately, many of these people have come to think of themselves as second-rate. Presidents also sometimes encounter a bureau-

J. L. Fisher and M. W. Tack (eds.). *Leaders on Leadership: The College Presidency.*
New Directions for Higher Education, no. 61. San Francisco: Jossey-Bass, Spring 1988.

cratic mentality of thoughtless egalitarianism, a resentment of those who strive to achieve beyond the comfortable and unthreatening norms of mediocrity. It is ironic that on many large urban campuses the very people who bemoan the lack of school spirit, and who have sunk to the depths of the "second-rate forever" mentality, are also the ones who criticize efforts to raise the university above the level of a parking lot with classrooms. Three critical issues faced by every president illustrate the importance of character and of commitment to the best long-term interests of the university.

Tenure-Track Appointments

The most important resource of any university is its faculty members—their quality, abilities, and motivation to excel. No university has ever completely avoided controversy over tenure decisions. It is hard to think of anything that can make a college president more disliked in the short term and more respected in the long term than his or her stand on tenure-track appointments and the granting of tenure. Experience clearly shows that the key decision is made at the time of an appointment, before a new faculty member has the opportunity to win friends among tenured faculty, who could let him or her escape close scrutiny when tenure recommendations are made.

To advance the university, a president must make tenure-track appointment decisions, or see that they are made, on a basis of absolute quality. In addition to demanding a high degree of demonstrated instructional effectiveness, juried scholarship, creative activity, and professional service, one must also ask the following questions: Has the person progressed in the chosen field to a level equal to or beyond that of others recently appointed ("equal to" if the department is of very high quality, and "beyond" if the department is below standard)? Is the candidate excited about the subject or bored with it? Is he or she committed or simply tired and coming to retire in the sun?

In too many public colleges and universities, presidents, vice-presidents, and deans occasionally relax standards on tenure to buy the fool's gold of popularity. If a president can be assured that a correct decision was made earlier at the faculty level, then the opportunity for lesser administrators to engage in popularity contests is diminished. A tenure decision can affect the university for the next thirty years. Barring resignation, early retirement, or death, a tenure decision may cost taxpayers up to $2 million in salary and benefits, provide an instructor for approximately six to seven thousand students, and prevent a more deserving person from occupying the position. When these stakes are considered, the stewardship responsibility of a president to the institution, to students, to taxpayers, and to faculty becomes clear.

Decision Making

One may ask why a president should make decisions at all. Why, instead of a single president, should there not be a management committee of ten faculty members? Quite apart from the legal accountability of the president to the trustees and of both the president and trustees to the state, the president is (or ought to be) at the center of a network of information. That network should include faculty, staff, students, alumni, and members of the community. The input should include knowledge of the best practices in higher education, whether gained from a study of the past or from curiosity about current practices elsewhere. It helps to have a sense of history; it is crucial to have an evolving vision of the future.

Some presidents visit faculty in their offices; some also hold visiting hours for students. Nervous bureaucrats in an administration may resent the insight and refinement of vision that is gained by presidents who visit faculty and receive students. Such bureaucrats may grumble about "getting outside the hierarchy." The president should, if he or she is to hear and work for good ideas and make informed and wise decisions. It is impossible for faculty to study all the issues and still have time to do the jobs they were hired to do.

Decisions are made on the basis of information available at the time. It is the responsibility of the president to ensure that decisions are made on the basis of the best information available at the time, in relation to the future of the institution. A president cannot be a passive receptor of the information that others decide he or she should see (often to further their own positions, or, as Miles's Law states, "Where you stand depends upon where you sit"). The president must ensure that there is a process to encourage the free flow of information in both directions and, whenever necessary, go beyond bureaucratic, hierarchical, constituent-group processing of information.

If consensus is possible, try it, but if you wait too long for it, you and the faculty will have at least one thing in common: old age. After a reasonable period, choices must be made. If they are wrong, cut your losses. If they are right, do not let criticism bother you.

Centers of Excellence

Given the enormous demands of the modern college presidency, it is difficult but imperative for the president to articulate a general vision of the future of the university, focus discretionary time on creating centers of excellence, and engage in continual personal self-renewal.

Articulating a general vision of the university's future consistently and forcefully may help to change the terms of debate. For example, the debate switches from whether there should be certain requirements to what the contents of required programs will be. If you do not set the agenda, you will merely be reacting to the issues of others.

By creating centers of excellence, one establishes levels to which the rest of the university community can aspire. A president must target money and people to create centers of excellence on campus. Those centers must be defended from the inevitable attacks by those who resent the quality for which they stand.

Most universities are not rich in resources. Thus, it is not possible to raise all departments to the same level of excellence. A university cannot flourish simply by supporting minimum performance in a thoughtless and leveling way. Even if one had the resources, differences between and within academic departments—in terms of creativity, proved accomplishments, talent, and potential—would still exist to a substantial degree.

With scarce resources and varied talents, one has to make choices about where limited funds will be invested. Do you put five new positions into a department that is not improving and where those five positions will only raise the quality of work from mediocre to below average? Or do you reward a few better departments by giving them positions that may raise them from being good to becoming excellent, and thus bring regional or national distinction to the university as a whole? These are the dilemmas that presidents face. Unfortunately, the modern-day levelers found on every campus have concluded that, no matter what the objective factors might be, one should simply divide the pie. As Montaigne wrote with reference to French education, "a little of everything and nothing well."

A tough provost, Frederick E. Terman, launched Stanford University on its road to distinction in the 1950s. Concentrating on peaks of excellence, he knew that quality attracted quality. He encouraged departmental heads to raise their sights and seek first-rate people. He knew that one cannot do everything at once, but that if enough departments start moving in the right direction, the pressure will increase on the others to catch up.

The president must also guard against the danger of leveling as the decision and the money carried to implement the decision flow downward. Beware of deans who simply react to the marching feet of undergraduates and to constant pressure from faculty. Just as corporate America faces pressures to appease stockholders on a quarterly, short-term basis, so also in the university there is the tendency to respond to the pressures of the moment and reallocate resources away from sound, long-term investments.

As a general rule, a president can achieve some key objectives by mandating allocations directly to units and constantly letting deans know what the philosophy of allocation is—for example, preserving an appropriate number of small-class experiences in a large university and encouraging integrative, capstone courses for majors. Needless to say, vice-presidents and deans who do act for the long-run should be appropriately compensated. (Some may even deserve "hazard pay," such as that awarded by some governments to people in career service who are assigned to hotter climates.)

Finally, if a president is going to encourage organizational and faculty renewal and advancement, the president's own personal renewal is also necessary. One must participate in national professional organizations that pertain to higher education or to one's discipline. By doing so, one gains a perspective beyond that derived from the daily life of the campus and comes in contact with different and often better ways of doing things. In the battle for quality, fresh ideas and character are the best weapons a president can have.

Taking the Risk

A college presidency can be lonely, but one cannot undertake it alone. Once one speaks out, previously silent allies are discovered to feel the same way. Often, these silent allies have not done much to support quality visibly against constant pressure from the levelers. Why not? Sometimes productive faculty shy away from tensions created in the various "sandboxes of campus politics," as one faculty member put it. They are busy in their classrooms and laboratories. Other times, no one has arranged a meeting to bring such faculty together. It takes time to mix the right faculty with each other and with the right professionals from the community. At California State University, Long Beach, the networks established by newer faculty and by 1,150 off-campus leaders, involved with forty-six school, departmental, and program advisory councils, have shown that it is time well spent. Interested deans and chairs are essential to the networking process, but if a president does not set the tone, perhaps few others will.

Too often, presidents become bored by repeating what they believe to be obvious. Be patient: You have heard yourself, but that does not mean others have heard you. They will not hear what you have to say unless you share your vision with them, encourage them, and enlist them to join you in taking the risks to move the university forward. If you do not do it, few others will. If you do, you can make a difference. Take the risk.

Stephen Horn, currently trustee professor of political science, served for eighteen years as president of California State University, Long Beach. He has also served as chair of the American Association of State Colleges and Universities.

Since conflict is inevitable, we should attempt to use it as a force for constructive change.

Making Conflict Work for You

Kenneth A. Shaw

It is usually assumed that presidents, chancellors, and others who hold major executive positions possess talents to cope with every situation. They are expected to be leaders in the truest sense. My intention here is to focus on one aspect of leadership with which few of us are realistically prepared to deal: conflict and its successful resolution.

Although we may wish it were otherwise, it is a fact of college and university administration that most of us spend much time dealing with conflict. We may find ourselves arbiters of disputes that have arisen among others. When we are asked or required to enter into the resolution of disputes among third parties, we must eventually make the final, binding decisions.

Most often, we join the advocates of a particular position in the very arena of conflict that we are attempting to bring under control. This is frequently the situation when one works with governmental agencies, boards of trustees, delegations that represent competing factions, and other groups. The leader must figuratively and often literally roll up his or her sleeves and get involved. To do otherwise is to miss a valuable opportunity for constructive change and to deal oneself out of the major decisions that must and will be made.

In this chapter, I will concentrate on practical advice for dealing with conflict and influencing its outcomes. These strategies and techniques have evolved during my experience as an academic dean, a uni-

J. L. Fisher and M. W. Tack (eds.). *Leaders on Leadership: The College Presidency.*
New Directions for Higher Education, no. 61. San Francisco: Jossey-Bass, Spring 1988.

versity president, and the chief executive of a statewide system of public higher education.

A Force for Constructive Change

The first and most important points to understand are that conflict must be viewed as inevitable; that, in most cases, conflict should also be viewed as constructive; and that it will be a constructive force if we take advantage of the opportunities it presents. Social institutions, at least in diverse societies, thrive on conflict, and a wise leader recognizes this.

Orson Welles, as Harry Lime in the classic British film, *The Third Man*, said, "Decades of warfare and bloodshed in medieval Italy produced the Renaissance. Five hundred years of peace, democracy, and brotherly love in Switzerland gave us the cuckoo clock." That, we hope, is an exaggeration, but it makes the point: Conflict is inevitable, and we should attempt to use it as a force for constructive change.

Adopting this attitude can help the leader deal more effectively with conflict. In those unavoidable periods when everything seems to be going wrong, it is an attitude that can help one maintain perspective and, perhaps, some inner peace.

Knowing the Outcomes of Conflict

It is essential that one be able to recognize the nature of the conflict with which he or she is dealing. There are three primary models of conflict, at least in a democratic society.

The Collegial Model. An important element of this model is the common goal of all parties involved in the dispute. The point of contention lies in conflicting expert judgments concerning the best ways to attain goals. In the end, the various parties involved in the conflict work together to fashion a resolution that is better than what any of them might have suggested individually. Everyone leaves delighted with both the process and the outcome.

Is this not how most faculty committees work? Think about recent committees dealing with general education, promotion, and tenure. Have they usually ended with consensus solutions better than those advanced by single parties? If your considered answer is no, then you have gained additional insight into the nature of most collegial disputes. We should certainly strive for the inspired synergistic consensus that is drawn from creative, group problem solving, but we should also be realistic about our chances. Each party to a conflict brings to the situation differing personal needs, values, and pressures. To believe that we can always achieve consensus solutions that are better than any advocated individually is certainly naive, probably destructive, and possibly dangerous. It is always worth attempting, however, and in a certain percentage of cases, it will succeed.

The Zero-Sum Model. This is the situation in checkers and football. Unfortunately, it also characterizes some of the deadlier games in which we must participate. Briefly described, the zero-sum model allows for only one winner; other parties to the dispute can only be unhappy with the outcome. Fortunately, zero-sum situations are not so common as some would have us believe.

You are in grave danger if you feel that all your conflicts must take this form, and you are in particular danger if you feel you must win them all. If you continually seem to be deeply embattled, perhaps your job is getting to you. In any event, I can guarantee that you have a lot of angry people around you.

If you have never been in a zero-sum situation, you have probably compromised issues, to no one's betterment. Solomon's solution of splitting the baby is hardly a practical method of dealing with day-to-day disputes (as most children and some parents would agree). Zero-sum situations do exist. For example, in public higher education there is constant pressure to entitle all state universities to offer doctoral programs, even when resources, needs, and common sense clearly suggest other decisions. The chief executive officer is better advised to resist this movement than to attempt watered-down compromise. In this case, a zero-sum solution, no matter how difficult, is required. Nevertheless, if you as a leader perceive that a problem is zero-sum in nature, it is crucially important for you to analyze and understand thoroughly your motivations at the outset. It is a signal of personal problems to see all conflicts in this way.

The Strategic Negotiation Model. Collective bargaining has made this model familiar to most of us, at least in concept. Clearly, this is the form of most conflicts with which we deal. This model is in our national tradition, as American as George Meany, Harry Truman, major-league sports, and faculty governance.

In the strategic negotiation model, each side will find it advantageous to yield somewhat. The goals of the various parties differ (unlike in the collegial model, where all parties share goals), but the participants understand that a negotiated outcome is preferable to a zero-sum outcome. One ought to admit, at least privately, that most decisions on college campuses are made according to this model. General education changes, for example, most certainly result from strategic negotiation.

Recall some conflicts to which you have been a party in recent years. Which were collegial? Which were zero-sum? Which were negotiated? Figure 1 shows my personal list.

Figure 1 shows that most outcomes were either negotiated or were reached by a combination of negotiation and the collegial process. A few outcomes were in the zero-sum category. These were no fun, but they had

Figure 1. Conflicts According to Model

Zero-Sum	Strategic Negotiation	Collegial
Certain resource and new-program decisions	General education changes	Enrollment management plan
Certain tenure decisions	Academic priorities	
	Strategic MIS plan	
	Revised admissions requirements	
	Revised transfer requirements	
	Catch-up faculty pay plan	
	Capital projects decisions	
	New budgets from legislatures and governors	

to be reached in this way, because the alternatives to dealing with them otherwise were even worse.

A most important point to remember is this: In constructing and studying your own list, you will become skillful at predicting the type of result you can expect. Regularly engaging in this exercise sharpens your ability to identify types of conflicts and their probable outcomes.

Techniques for Conflict Resolution

Regardless of the type of conflict, there are specific techniques for resolving it. These techniques are effective, whether the executive has to resolve differences between others or is actually involved in the conflict. Thus, they can help to resolve interdepartmental disputes as well as interpersonal differences. They are even more valuable, because they gain potency as they are shared with others, especially with those in adversarial positions. If adversaries are aware of and use these techniques, mutually advantageous solutions are likely outcomes. Their successful use, however, requires the following steps to occur in the sequence presented here. Over time, it may be possible to drop the second step, but not until relationships are so strong that each party knows the other is listening. The other three steps must never be excluded.

Listen. Listening is a skill that must be learned and learned well, and it does not come easily. It is particularly difficult for harried executives, untrained in its practice and unaware of its importance. We must overcome the tendency to think about what we will say next while the other person is talking. Listening is essential in dealing effectively with conflict. To be certain that we understand what is important to the other party, we need the information we gather from listening. Furthermore, an effective listener allows his or her adversary to relax—to deal with issues, rather than with personalities—and to focus on constructive solutions.

Repeat What Has Been Said. Paraphrase the positions of the other parties, according to your understanding. This step allows you to verify your perceptions of other positions. If you have misconstrued a person's words or body language (and one should never underestimate the importance of nonverbal communication in such exchanges), you now have the opportunity to correct your understanding. Repeating what you have just heard is also the most effective way possible to communicate that you are listening, that you do care what others think, and that you want to work things out. In short, it creates a positive climate for dealing with differences.

Indicate Areas of Agreement. This step is important because it encourages adversaries to set aside spurious issues, enabling them to focus more specifically on the issues that should be discussed and saving time and emotional energy. Beyond that, it creates a positive climate for resolving real differences, rather than imaginary ones. By identifying areas of mutual harmony at this early stage, all parties can see that agreements far outnumber disagreements; this is certainly the usual case. Identifying agreements underscores the desirability of resolving differences and realizing the common good.

Indicate Areas of Disagreement. This is the time to begin resolving differences. If all parties are using a shared technique, issues are clearly defined, and a format is established for their resolution.

Arbitrating Third-Party Disputes

When you are called on to render a decision—that is, to settle a difference—between other parties, there are some helpful guidelines you may wish to apply. These follow from the four conflict-resolution steps.

Contentious staff members often want to unload their concerns about adversaries' positions on policy, technique, process, and so on. Their visits with you almost guarantee that you will soon be talking with their adversaries. Rather than invest valuable time in listening to allegations, you might try saying: "I understand that there are these differences. Before we go any farther, let me suggest that you outline your position—in writing, if necessary. Discuss it with Bill, and ask him to present his position. Before you come back to me, I want you to determine the areas where you agree and those that remain unresolved. I would like to know the results of these discussions. If disagreements

58

remain, bring them to me. I will meet with the two of you and settle them very quickly."

I have found that this approach frequently results in mutually agreeable settlements without my further intervention. The last thing the contending parties usually want is a decision on a matter of such personal importance to be made by a busy president who is uninterested in hearing the details. When I have been required to make final decisions, the contending parties have at least identified mechanisms for resolving future disputes.

Conflict can be a positive force for change, and we must recognize its attributes. We must attempt to determine which type of conflict is involved and which outcomes are most likely. We should then apply the four steps that can lead to its resolution. The more disputants are aware of and use these techniques, the greater the prospects for mutually agreeable outcomes.

Following this advice will not guarantee your success, nor will it guarantee that your days as president will be free from stress. View these suggestions as useful tools. With your other strong leadership skills and your deep commitment, they will help ensure that your tenure in office will produce lasting improvements for your institution. This achievement will be a source of continuing pride and will reaffirm your wisdom in electing this career path. Remember, too, when things get very difficult, conflict is inevitable. Good luck.

Kenneth A. Shaw is president of the University of Wisconsin system.

Survival and effective service in the presidency are possible when the incumbent retains basic human qualities, fits the institution, and balances pitfalls with satisfactions.

Keeping Presidents Fully Alive

E. K. Fretwell, Jr.

There is a legend that the late humorist Robert Benchley, as an undergraduate at Harvard, faced an examination question requiring him to discuss the Newfoundland fisheries from a particular point of view. He chose to do so from that of the fish. In similar fashion, the following discussion will focus on the college presidency largely from the point of view of the incumbent—old or young, experienced or otherwise—as a human being.

During the campus unrest of the Vietnam War period in the early 1970s, campus graffiti were rife. My favorite was a seven-word admonition scrawled on an Oberlin College sidewalk: BEING HUMAN ISN'T HARD—WHY NOT TRY? The real challenge inherent in the presidency is surviving with honor and decency to get the job done as well as possible, while bringing to it human qualities that enhance the performance of colleagues and all those whom the institution serves. Ideally, the incumbent becomes an even better person in the process and occasionally even has a little fun along the way. The president has a responsibility to stay fully alive—professionally, intellectually, and humanly.

Today's world is confusing and dangerous; tomorrow's could be even more so. The university, however defined, has a unique role to play in increasing intellectual and human opportunities. Drawing selectively from the past, it helps all who would learn and expand current knowledge to interpret the present and prepares citizens as well as skilled prac-

J. L. Fisher and M. W. Tack (eds.). *Leaders on Leadership: The College Presidency.*
New Directions for Higher Education, no. 61. San Francisco: Jossey-Bass, Spring 1988.

titioners for the years ahead. Those chosen to lead the university are in a positive position to work creatively with others to achieve these goals.

If the president's role could be summarized in a single sentence, we might say that it involves actively putting ideas, people, and other resources together to reach clearly defined goals. The trinity of teaching, research, and public service is the usually cited outcome. The institution as Wriston (1959) has noted, should "be a place and an instrument to promote human growth by the human effort of teacher and taught" (pp. 131–132). His definition still holds, especially at the undergraduate level.

Although very little direct classroom teaching in most institutions is done by the president, his or her influence is felt through a variety of means (including suggestions, direction, reward allocations, and appointment of personnel), which can be viewed as indirect forms of teaching. Presidents, like managers, serve as trouble-shooters and supervisors but are of only limited value unless they take seriously their role of identifying and then planning for the future of the institution (Dimock, 1945, p. 24). Effective selection of the president is vital. In most cases, boards of trustees appoint to the presidency men and women with good records and earmarks of likely success, based on such factors as intelligence, disciplined ambition, integrity, and the ability to learn and grow on the job.

Why do some succeed while others do not? Luck plays a part (Kerr, 1984), but there is far more to it than that. Many observers agree that university administration is an art, as well as a science. In my own experience, both actual and vicarious, three aspects of the presidency add up to achievement and longevity: having or developing the right style for the particular institution; avoiding pitfalls, both local and general; and identifying and utilizing appropriate rewards.

The Right Style

Administering a college or a university is like sailing a boat. Using the available wind (resources) in the most advantageous manner, and plotting an achievable—perhaps even daring—course, one may reach desirable destinations. The true leader draws on past experience and assesses current conditions to determine what works in a particular human and institutional context.

Two factors are absolutely vital: a superb sense of timing, and a realization that sometimes people respond not so much to objective facts, but rather to their perceptions of what is happening. The successful executive needs to sense when the faculty or the student body, or both, are ready to move ahead in a particular direction and when they are not. Development of a new set of faculty or student bylaws may seem like a routine task, but frequently it is not. When the several segments of a campus community have reached the point of perceiving changes as positive, action can go forward fruitfully and quickly. If, however, the perception prevails that a heavy-handed administration is trying to rush something through, a digging in of heels may occur. Up to some logical limit, administrative patience is desirable.

Openness of style is also very important. Many faculty people think access to top decision makers is essential. Although the president obviously cannot discuss everything with everybody all the time, his or her participation in a certain amount of discussion with campus colleagues before making important decisions can ease the shock of change. Even though well-defined institutional rules set by the governing board can make it clear to all that the president has complete executive authority, the wise leader does not flaunt this authority excessively. Effective contracts for collective bargaining, where they exist, unambiguously define the president's role.

The president must of necessity delegate authority in many matters, while retaining the right of final approval, but must also stand ready to explain official decisions when they are questioned. Among the tougher decisions are how to allocate insufficient funds, how to terminate as gracefully and fairly as possible faculty or staff who are not deemed to be good long-term investments for the institution, and how to say no to those who seek institutional endorsement of or support for inappropriate external causes.

Being constantly in touch with major institutional issues and viewpoints, without being engulfed by them, is also necessary. Informal walks around campus, accessibility in the cafeteria (not, however, for long, serious debates), and occasional office hours for interested campus persons are worthwhile aspects of openness. To make such activities possible on an endurable schedule, the president must have devoted and tactful assistants in his or her office. Physical and mental endurance, together with a sense of humor (often with an ironic twist), are absolutely essential.

Major Pitfalls

The president must relate to everybody but belong to nobody. His or her role resembles that of a tightrope artist. Ideally, the president is respected (but not necessarily loved) by the faculty; admired or at least tolerated by the trustees, as well as by the central office of a multicampus system; and accepted as a champion of students, the alumni, and the community in which the campus is situated. All this respect, admiration, and acceptance notwithstanding, the first pitfall to avoid is any belief on the part of the president that he or she is irreplaceable. Other mistakes include the following:

- Taking oneself too seriously
- Not taking the presidency seriously enough
- Being habitually unable to differentiate between the position of president and the individual filling it (I once knew a president who helped design a campus building and then perceived any criticism of it as a personal attack)
- Becoming overcome by fatigue, boredom, or the lack of those intellectual or personal satisfactions that help bring about a balanced view of life
- Overreacting to small concerns ("I can't stand these petty insults!") or failing to defend the institution on big issues
- Being excessively discouraged that one's institution is not perceived as a "flagship," or feeling lofty because it is
- Failing to take advantage of organizations or networks that can provide advice when it is sought, solace when it is needed, and true companionship over the long haul.

An admonition: The truly effective and dedicated president takes on responsibility not only for the welfare of the institution but also, in a sense, for the welfare of heads of other colleges and universities. Taking a telephone call from another president who needs to talk is part of the job. Presidents probably comprise the best of all possible support systems for one another.

Rewards and Satisfactions

On balance, despite its occasional darker aspects, the presidency can be a source of great personal and professional satisfaction, provided its tasks are undertaken with decorum and at least some modesty. When I was about to leave my first presidency, after over eleven years, the incoming acting president sought my sense of that office as compared with the academic vice-presidential post she then occupied. My response was, "The lows are lower, but the highs are higher."

Desirable salaries and benefits for presidents continue, appropriately, to receive attention; but one benefit honored more in the breach than in the observance is the professional-development leave. Most good universities have long since adopted the idea of sabbatical leaves for faculty members. The president—often on call twenty-four hours a day for eleven months of the year and, even on vacation, seldom out of telephone range—can also use intellectual, professional, and personal leave. Time with family and friends is important. The growing body of literature on presidents and their spouses, for example, should become increasingly known to policymakers who are trustees and heads of university systems. A fresh approach is needed periodically. Some university systems might do well to use informal arrangements for rotating administrators from campuses to central offices, and vice versa.

What can the president do to stay fully alive for both the short and the long run?

1. Read regularly—original scholarship, the more important literature about higher education, and other material just for fun.
2. Attempt a program of regular daily exercise (a brisk early-morning walk holds particular appeal for me).
3. Build in rewards along the way—a twenty-minute escape to the library, a scheduled quiet evening at home, a visit to a theatrical or musical performance or to a stimulating museum after a fatiguing professional trip.
4. Serve, as appropriate, in local, regional, and national organizations or commissions that meet the test of being worthwhile and nonperfunctory and provide contact with stimulating people.

Significant studies of the role of college and university presidents and their "many lives" have been stimulated by the Commission on Strengthening Presidential Leadership sponsored by the Association of Governing Boards of Universities and Colleges. In the words of Kerr and Gade (1986), presidents continue to operate in a challenging "series of environments, most marked by a context of confusion about goals, of inconsistent pressures for action and no action, of substantial constraints, and of opportunities small and great but occasionally nonexistent" (p. 3).

American higher education faces an increasingly demanding future, and we watch the urgency of better leadership become increasingly evident. As Newman (1987) reminds us, "The improvement of the quality of a university does not just happen" (p. 92). Leadership is needed from the president as never before, and this leadership for the future must be characterized more and more in terms of cooperative endeavors. "Cooperation—not competition: This is the new challenge for leadership in higher education" (National Commission on the Role and Future of State Colleges and Universities, 1986, p. 37).

Goals such as these can be reached if true leaders can be identified, inducted, and induced to remain on the job long enough to achieve them. Style, avoidance of pitfalls, and the nurturance of reasonable and satisfying rewards can help institutions retain such leaders. Trustees, governors, system officers, and the public generally—all of whom care about the success of colleges and universities and of their leaders—might take seriously Benchley's approach to the Newfoundland fisheries: Consider the big issues from the viewpoint of the fish.

References

Dimock, M. E. *The Executive in Action.* New York: Harper & Row, 1945.
Kerr, C. *Presidents Make a Difference: Strengthening Leadership in Colleges and Universities.* Washington, D.C.: Association of Governing Boards of Universities and Colleges (AGB), 1984.

64

Kerr, C., and Gade, M. *The Many Lives of Academic Presidents: Time, Place, and Character.* Washington, D.C.: AGB, 1986.

National Commission on the Role and Future of State Colleges and Universities. *To Secure the Blessings of Liberty.* Washington, D.C.: American Association of State Colleges and Universities, 1986.

Newman, F. *Choosing Quality: Reducing Conflict between the State and the University.* Denver, Colo.: Education Commission of the States, 1987.

Wriston, H. M. *Academic Procession.* New York: Columbia University Press, 1959.

E. K. Fretwell, Jr., current chancellor of the University of North Carolina at Charlotte and chair of the Council on Postsecondary Accreditation, also served as president of the State University College at Buffalo.

The president is the university's chief strategist.

The President's Game

George W. Johnson

Having been president at only one university, my perspective is necessarily narrow, but it seems to me that the presidency is one of the great jobs to hold in our time, if you can enter it with a certain abandon and a willingness to careen a bit.

The way I see the presidency depends, of course, on how I see the world. For the past two decades, I have been feeling that I am living through a turbulent transition in the world's history. I have been privileged (or cursed) to participate in a whole series of social revolutions. As an academician, I have been at the center of much of the turbulence. I saw a cultural consensus, on which my education and my teaching had always depended, begin to collapse and disintegrate in the 1960s. I saw the nature of cities change before my eyes, as what we have now learned to call networks of urban villages began to emerge as prototypes of urban organization.

These changes were disintegrative; they undercut all the imaginative constructs on which my thinking depended. Moreover, they threatened the emotional base of my ability to function as a social being: I had grown up as the son of immigrant parents, who were imbued with notions of the melting pot and who were sure that a poor boy could rise and better himself. Finally and slowly—since I am not a business executive, an economist, or a politician—I began to sense that the whole economic basis of my society was shifting away from things to people, from

J. L. Fisher and M. W. Tack (eds.). *Leaders on Leadership: The College Presidency.*
New Directions for Higher Education, no. 61. San Francisco: Jossey-Bass, Spring 1988.

the mighty and sometimes colossal machines that amplified puny human muscle to the increasingly enigmatic machines that amplified but also threatened the powers of the human mind.

The scene was certainly fascinating; but, as one after another of our social institutions shifted or mutated, it became clear to me that education, too, must change. Still when one's whole identity is called into question, it is not easy to contemplate changes, and it is even harder to act. Judging from my own experience, I would guess that it was about this time, in the early 1970s, that colleges and universities began to lose the critical detachment that had been their defining characteristic. Perhaps a storm-cellar mentality was our natural sanctuary; in any case, we became increasingly intolerant of threatening ideas and less able to watch ourselves with amusement and humility.

Whereas in the 1950s we had identified corporate business with a lack of self-awareness, in the 1980s we began to see a complete reversal of that notion. Corporate offices are now often hotbeds of ideas and intellectual discourse, while universities are increasingly scholastic, self-contained, and unintellectual (if we define an intellectual as one capable of watching himself or herself think). With every passing month and every new report on educational reform or improvement, our own lack of self-awareness becomes more evident. Most academicians, for instance, know about higher education's history, but they are not really conscious that the organizational characteristics of their institutions were all invented after the Civil War: the academic department, the undergraduate college as we think of it, the graduate school, the professional-school training format, and even the semester credit hour. These developments coincided with the expansion of industrial America. Indeed, if we match our synchronous, serial approach to undergraduate education with the methods of early production lines, we can see that we are the last institution in the country to retain the factory system (even American factories do not really use it any longer). We work, that is, in an artifact of the industrial age.

It is an obvious paradox of human behavior that people become least anxious to rock the boat as it approaches the waterfall. At such a time, most of us in the academy know better than to stand up and speak too loudly of the turbulence ahead; indeed, a few will even try to pretend that all is well, to oil the oarlocks and sing loudly against the roar of the water. Of course, those of us who are college presidents try not to let our boats get into that position in the first place. But what can we do? If, despite the daily avalanche of memos, we still like to see ourselves as speculative thinkers, it is fun to play the part of Jeremiah. Nevertheless, visions ought not to be a university president's preoccupation. I must say that I have never had one. I am just not very good at looking over the horizon. I do not really like to bet much of my own money on my own prophecies, and I find that when the stakes are real, any vision I have tends to fade even as my palms sweat. I know today I would not follow someone who is subject to visions, nor would I really expect anyone else to follow me if I had them.

Instead, as president, I am my institution's chief game player, its strategist, its general planner, and planning general. Strategic planning has, of course, been talked about in higher education administration for almost a decade, but most strategic plans that I see are simply wish lists ("Within five years, we will become among the top institutions in the field of . . . "). Wistful and pretentious longings are not plans. Plans rest on assessments of your opposition and its weaknesses, of your opportunities and strengths, and of the grounds for exploitation. Thinking that way is easier to describe than to do, but you have an enormous advantage if you work at an emerging institution like mine, an upstart in the educational establishment, a parvenu whose pretensions threaten Western civilization and the size of the flagship's portion of the budgetary pie. At a rising state institution that challenges the flagship universities, you can count on having a full range of opposition—in fact, one of the central facts of life at a regional state university is the unremitting hostility expressed by the educational establishment. As president of such an institution, your job is not to wish eloquently, but to maneuver precisely—to position the university.

Considering the usual nature of the opposition, it is useful to make a distinction between bureaucratic and entrepreneurial planning. Most bureaucratic planners—this group includes people in many universities and failing businesses, and certainly staffs of state education councils—depend on an assumed continuity and tend to plan in linear projections, always constrained by rationality. (Indeed, as it ages, a bureaucratic office spends an increasing amount of energy justifying its own past, covering the abrupt hiatus and the jagged progression, attempting always to smooth the facts into a predictable, intelligible, and unthreatening curve.) Entrepreneurial planners, in contrast, assume discontinuity and anticipate change, although they make no pretense of predicting it (if this were possible, one would do better to stay at the race track). The bureaucrat assumes that change can be kept at the periphery of the enterprise and will not affect core purposes, while the entrepreneur assumes that change is part of the enterprise itself. Against change, the potentially destructive element, the bureaucrat attempts to build a higher sea wall; the entrepreneur looks for a better surfboard.

To be a strategist, you need not envision or predict much. You do have to take responsibility for the campaign, however, and for its results. You can be bold and dashing, or you can be ponderous and methodical. What counts is whether the dominant hills are occupied and the critical fords seized. Defining the institution's strategy for development seems to me to be the university president's chief task during times like ours;

indeed, I cannot imagine the chief executive officer doing anything else happily or effectively.

By way of illustration, let me use my own situation. George Mason University was a new, regional, state-supported university in northern Virginia, which was something of a sophisticated frontier populated by affluent, highly educated, and cosmopolitan citizens who were viewed as transient and undependable by the rest of the commonwealth. In the state's scheme of things, our institution was assigned a mission of the second or third order and was expected to stay there. To break out of that confining assignment, the university had to risk being a troublemaker and a political problem. Its strategy was fairly simple: It had to earn and keep the allegiance and support of its region, use that political base to position itself as a special institution for the entire state, and use the support earned in the latter role to drive its programs to a level of national distinction. The university had to achieve some national distinction before it could earn the allegiance of its very sophisticated region, but it had to have that allegiance before it could garner the support necessary to attract nationally eminent scholars.

This cycle could have been a defeating vicious circle if we had not found a special strength and a special weakness to exploit. It was waiting for us in the issue of economic development. The high-tech business community of the region began to realize not only that it required the kind of stimulating intellectual environment only a major university can provide, but also that industry was becoming increasingly vital to the entire Virginia economy. With the sometimes impassioned support of the business community, George Mason University was able to pursue its strategy effectively.

In the course of doing so, the university and its president learned something; and, in some sense, the history of the institution is one of self-discovery. What we learned was that the university's salvation lay in its giving up self-regard and becoming other-centered. We learned that a university-business partnership cannot hope to thrive if it is university-centered, if it depends on what the university would like to do for business and on what it would like to extract from business. Instead, it must be centered on the needs of business, which business itself is often unable to articulate and examine, an inability that lays the groundwork for a genuinely collaborative exploration with its university partner. In that collaboration, the university gains vitality from its exposure to another reality. Equally important, it engages the active participation, not just the passive advice, of a powerful ally. After two decades of breakup and fragmentation, our society desperately needs a focus for community building, and very few of our social institutions are really well positioned to take central responsibility for that effort. To the degree that it can avoid self-interest, the university has an enormous opportunity to fill the void.

The university, however, can hardly hope to involve itself in building communities unless it achieves a degree of wholeness itself. To a large extent, academicians have forgotten the habits of holistic thinking. An intense emphasis on self-development, a legacy of the 1960s, has become common among many faculty members, so that priorities and management are viewed as inimical, and the ideal academic state is considered to be one in which one hundred flowers are allowed to bloom without direction or constraint. Faculty senates are poorly attended, conflicts of interest that once would have been abhorrent are now widely ignored, and collective responsibilities (as opposed to prerogatives) tend to be shunned.

What can a university president do to help? If the president enjoys preaching, or demonstrating to the faculty that he or she can still think, it is possible to indulge in more or less strenuous exhortation. If he or she enjoys this, probably no great harm is done, but I have really grave doubts about the ability of any president to talk out consensus. I also doubt that much is accomplished by letting the grass grow and relying on administrative decentralization. Neither approach works very well without some general allegiance to the core values of the institution, and I do not believe that any sizable institution retains such values. Whatever consensus faculty groups achieve is almost inevitably self-serving, rather than other-centered.

The institutional president must depend on positioning. He or she must do everything possible to open the realities of academic life to the realities of the marketplace, the things of the mind to the things of the mundane, jarring as many people as possible out of the conventional wisdom on which both realities depend. Once such openings occur, the president should foster experiment—curricular experiment, organizational experiment, whatever—not to find solutions for given problems (although he or she may stumble on one), but to bring faculty and staff face-to-face with their common problems. At the same time, the president ought to recruit restive people from outside the institution, give them as much scope as possible, and turn them loose. There is always the chance that one such individual will find the way home—in which case the president can always run before him or her and reclaim the role of leader. Above all, the president should seize every opportunity to cause trouble, to make the conventional path more trouble than the unconventional one, to place the retention of time-honored organization in the path of some newly ignited heart's desire. In addition, the president should do whatever he or she can—through public relations, speeches, and general posture—to build up a sense of institutional momentum.

Posture, stance, attitude—these are as important as vision and dreams. Every new president ought to be counseled to take advantage of his or her "honeymoon." Presidents may not really know yet what they are talking about, but that has almost nothing to do with their effectiveness during this period. People are not really listening to presidents' speeches during the honeymoon, but to their body language. People want to watch a player. In our time, to be responsible and to have any hope of being effective, a university president must simply want to play the game.

George W. Johnson is president of George Mason University, Fairfax, Virginia.

The life of a college president can be fun; it can kill; it can be eternally frustrating—but it also can provide an inner satisfaction that few other professions afford.

Changing Roles and New Expectations

Prezell R. Robinson

It is reasonably clear to most individuals who have occupied the presidential office during the past fifteen years that their roles and expectations have changed dramatically. Suffice it to say that those in the grandstand—some faculty, trustees, alumni, and students—have from time to time romanticized the presidency as a position for an erudite scholar, whose every word reflects broad training in philosophy, history, religion, languages, and the sciences. Perhaps in the earlier days of higher education, presidents were glorified and content; then, too, opportunities abounded for reflective thinking, and there was time for research and the occasional presentation of scholarly papers. Certainly, some of these opportunities and expectations still exist, but they certainly are not as prevalent as they were twenty-five or thirty years ago. The truth of the matter is that at many of our small, church-related, nonprestigious institutions, the president is not only expected to lead but to be a jack of all trades. Leading in such an environment is certainly tricky. Leadership means different things to different constituencies.

The president must be able to communicate effectively with his or her board, soothe the psychic wounds of some influential alumni, become a fundraiser par excellence, and keep students happy, especially at homecoming and other strictly social affairs. Fisher (1984) has said, "The

J. L. Fisher and M. W. Tack (eds.). *Leaders on Leadership: The College Presidency.*
New Directions for Higher Education, no. 61. San Francisco: Jossey-Bass, Spring 1988.

president is expected to perform as a master of everything—an effective combination of Abraham Lincoln, John F. Kennedy, Queen Elizabeth I, and Mother Teresa" (p. 3).

A dentist generally spends four years in college, another three to four years in dental school, and perhaps a year as an intern; a doctor follows a similar career path. The architect and the engineer generally pursue training designed to equip them to carry out their professional responsibilities effectively. As Riesman (1978) noted, however, there is no specific career line that prepares one for the college or university presidency. Indeed, the notion still exists in some quarters that the college presidency is a peaceful, rather static position that has not changed substantially over the years. Using the 1926 Lowell lectures at Harvard as his foundation, Whitehead (1966) indicated that throughout recorded history people have thought, built, and acted as though each generation of leaders would essentially live under conditions similar to those of their ancestors and that they would transmit these same conditions to their children. Moreover, he implied that we are living in the first period of time when this notion may be false. Whitehead also conveyed the idea that the accelerated rate of change today has an impact on leadership qualities such as objectivity, flexibility, and resiliency. These comments anticipate the situation in which some college presidents find themselves today.

Accordingly, no matter what problems confront an institution, the president is expected to handle them. In numerous situations, new presidents, many of whom have been departmental heads, deans, and administrative assistants, find themselves totally unprepared for the rude awakening they experience when they are thrust into a presidency.

In recent years, some observers have noted the exit of an increased number of presidents from their positions in the academy. I recently attended a meeting of presidents of historically black colleges, where over 50 percent of the presidents had been in their positions for less than three years. Of course, there are similar problems at other institutions.

Consider these lines by Miles (1973):

A man arrived at the Pearly Gate. His face was scarred and old.
He stood before the Gate of Fate for admission to the fold.
"What have you done," Saint Peter asked, "to gain admission here?"
"I've been a college president, sir, for many and many a year."
The Pearly Gate swung open wide, and Saint Peter touched the bell.
"Come in," he said, "and choose your harp; you've had your taste of hell" [p. 4].

Presidents, as leaders, must lead, but if leaders march too far ahead of those being led, followers fall by the wayside. If leaders march too closely to followers, however, sometimes followers march over them. As Brown (1979) so aptly put it: "A leader has to be able to convey to those around him that he has a sense of vision and knows the direction in which the institution is going. . . . He must be able to sift out of the various alternatives those which are important directions. He must see these in advance; he must be able to predict problem areas over the forces and winds of change. If he cannot do this, he and his institution will be off balance. It is like steering a ship and keeping it on course" (p. 6).

Problems do indeed exist in the administration of small, church-related, historically black colleges. On the basis of my twenty-one years as president of such an institution in the South, I also believe there are some demonstrable differences in role expectations and opportunities. To elaborate further:

1. These colleges are very likely to be grossly underfinanced, with infinitesimally small endowments. This situation requires a special kind of assertive leadership from the president.
2. A fairly large segment of the total community feels strongly that these institutions are fundamentally and basically inferior. Leaders in this situation must convince the larger community that support for one of these colleges is a sound investment.
3. In many cases, the view prevails that leaders of these colleges simply should expect less support than the majority institutions. Unquestionably, presidents of these colleges generally do not have access to the coffers, nor do they often have the access to affluent citizens that chief executive officers of majority institutions can depend on.

In fairness, I should say there does seem to be a slowly evolving concept, especially in corporate America, that there is a need for these colleges to have first-rate leadership, because they represent a vital part of a great pluralistic society and are therefore vital to the national interest.

During my tenure as president, I have discovered some general guidelines that enhance the possibility of success.

1. The president must establish an effective relationship with his or her board, alumni, the larger community, parents, and students.
2. The president must learn early to delegate authority to his or her deans and other administrative officers.
3. The president should make a conscious effort to seek out the very best faculty and staff he or she can find, especially when appointing a chief fiscal officer, a chief academic officer, a chief development officer, and a chief of student affairs.

4. There simply is no substitute for an enlightened, deeply committed board of trustees, and the chief executive officer must seek out the very best trustees he or she can find. Other things being equal, several wealthy individuals certainly would not hurt.
5. Early in his or her tenure, the president should try to establish a reputation as an effective manager of fiscal affairs.
6. With the support and encouragement of his or her board and faculty, the president should make a conscious effort to produce competitive graduates.
7. With the support and involvement of the board, faculty, staff, students, and alumni, the president should constantly review the mission of the college. He or she should also develop strategies to guide the institution successfully toward its stated goals. Furthermore, he or she must gain from faculty a strong commitment to the attainment of those goals.

The twenty-one years I have spent at Saint Augustine College have been among the most rewarding of my life. I have gained much satisfaction from putting together a first-rate board and securing the best administrative officers and faculty our resources could command. If I were starting out anew, a college presidency would still be high on my list of job opportunities to seek.

References

Brown, D. G. *Leadership Validity: A Workbook for Academic Administration.* Washington, D.C.: American Council on Education, 1979.
Fisher, J. L. *Power of the Presidency.* New York: ACE/Macmillan, 1984.
Miles, D. Speech presented at Immaculata College, Immaculata, Pa., 1973.
Riesman, D. "Beyond the '60s." *Wilson Quarterly,* 1978, *2,* 59–71.
Whitehead, A.W.N. *Religion in the Making.* Cleveland, Ohio: Meridian Books, 1966.

Prezell R. Robinson is president of Saint Augustine College, Raleigh, North Carolina.

Leadership is like love. We cannot define it or teach it, yet we can always identify it.

Love Me, Lead Me, and Leave Me Alone

Judith S. Eaton

I became a college president because I had hope. We are, after all, a viable, valuable society, in which the positive dimensions of being human can be encouraged. Education, I thought, is the essential enabling activity by which this process can occur. I even envisioned presidential leadership in education as making a difference. I believed in the primacy of the individual and put great faith in enhancing individual capacity for independent action and thought. I also thought that individual capacity for sensitivity and concern for others would be encouraged, and that social improvement would result from the growth of the individual.

Many years later, my hope is not so strong. Is leadership—the capacity to mobilize resources, to get things done—important to the enhancing of individual capacity? Can an organization (a college or a university) make a difference for individuals? I even ask myself whether a meaningful college presidency is possible in a society whose perception of leadership is, to say the least, confused.

Leadership Approaches and Issues

Colleges and universities are seen in our society as organizations with a conflicting and important array of tasks. We create the future, we

J. L. Fisher and M. W. Tack (eds.). *Leaders on Leadership: The College Presidency.*
New Directions for Higher Education, no. 61. San Francisco: Jossey-Bass, Spring 1988.

determine values, and we provide the focus as well as the direction of human intellectual effort. Why else is Bloom (1987) so concerned? It is precisely because, in the United States of America, the intellectual growth and development of our citizens is profoundly and almost exclusively connected to our colleges and universities. We value the idea of these institutions highly, and we put faith in their effectiveness.

The pace of change in our society, the present limited capacity of government, our confusion concerning democracy and direction, the ascendancy of individualism—all these trends have affected our expectations of colleges and universities. A further complication is our economic circumstances. Clearly, it is not an easy time for colleges and universities. It is not an easy time to attempt leadership of such organizations, nor is it an easy time for education itself.

In general, we find two approaches to presidential leadership in our colleges and universities. These approaches reflect extremes in thinking, and they occupy opposite ends of a continuum. They are rarely present in pure form in any collegiate leadership situation. They can be combined to produce other approaches, such as political or bureaucratic models of leadership. We shall call them the *authoritarian* and the *collegial* approaches to leadership. They are important because they are fundamental.

The authoritarian approach is based on two notions: that people must be led, and that leaders must do the leading. Leaders are required to marshal the forces of an organization, to stimulate effort, to capture imagination, to inspire, and to serve as models for sustained effort. The authoritarian approach allows people to identify leaders as the causes of events. It diminishes the discomfort that might emerge from the failure to understand the reasons for what occurs.

The collegial approach is based on a different premise: that people do not need to be led. Indeed, according to this approach, leadership is most effective when people set their own goals, pick their own activities, and have freedom of choice. In this approach, good leaders tend not to lead, but to be helpful. Thus, leadership is only one of several variables affecting the life of an organization. The most effective leader is a catalyst, a resource; he or she permits group strength and individual responsibility.

It is not enough to describe approaches to leadership, however. It is important to go farther in our thinking. What are we attempting to achieve through presidential leadership? What are the purposes of our institutions and their leadership? At the most general level, we want well-managed institutions, to provide the nation with intellectual opportunity and direction. Our institutions exist primarily for the cognitive, conceptual, and theoretical growth of our citizens and our society. This ideal is easy to state, but it is very difficult to achieve. As I assess our present circumstances, I detect three areas of extraordinary concern, which can compromise effective presidential leadership: the present nature of change, our contemporary concept of individual freedom, and our current sense of organizational autonomy. They complicate the realization of our purposes.

Whether this perception is actually true or not, change does appear to be increasingly out of control. *USA Today* and "Cable Network News" may keep us superficially informed, but they also keep us uncertain. One way to describe the impact of change is to point to the growing perception that the domains of individual action are increasingly unstable, discontinuous, and unsafe. Simultaneously, our sense of weakened capacity to control our own affairs affects our perceptions of acceptable leadership. We are not sure what forms of leadership are safe. In general, we respond by resisting change, instead of attempting to dominate the factors that influence change. Are we also afraid?

What is individual freedom, in a world of large organizations, multinational conglomerates, and government through vested-interest groups? Even our representative democracy appears increasingly obsolete, because of our electronic access to direct decision making. What is individual freedom, in a cacophony of voices and opinions, and in the absence of any framework for evaluating, supporting, or denying these voices? A society for which any and all approaches to standards and values are considered equal has failed to take on its fundamental responsibility: determining an intellectual and ethical framework for its future. There are instances in which all approaches are not equal, circumstances in which the principle of equality is inappropriate. We are confused about individual freedom.

Organizational freedom focuses, in this instance, on the prerogatives of a college or a university, rather than on those of its constituents. After taking into account board members, students, faculty, administrators, other staff members, and the community, there is still the institution. It is more than its constituents. It has enormous symbolic value. It is uniquely the responsibility of the chief executive officer. We have yet to address our sense of shared responsibility for the preservation of individual and organizational freedom. Rather, we prefer to see the assertion of organizational prerogatives, always at the price of the individual, and the assertion of individual prerogatives at the price of the organization. We are generally suspicious of organizational freedom.

Leadership Behavior and Expectations

What do we do? How do we deal with these extraordinary concerns and yet realize effective leadership? Perhaps my hope about presidential leadership will be sustained if I rephrase the question: "What is leadership?"

There is much thoughtful writing concerning the nature of the relationship between leaders and those whom they lead: the leader-constituent issue. There are also careful considerations of leadership as a system. Most of these discussions, however insightful, leave me with the idea that the primary function of leadership is continual negotiation with institutional constituencies (accompanied by the refrain "lead me, but leave me alone"). Indeed, much of the leadership literature reflects ambivalence about the expression of authority.

Rather than attempt definitions, it would be more fruitful to focus on expectations of leadership. What should leaders do, and how should they do it? What standards of leadership behavior are desirable?

Leaders are, at least in part, the creations of those whom they lead. What we expect of leadership style and substance says a good deal about our social values and about the leadership we will get. Thus, leadership reflects the values of a society, both good and bad, and leadership quality is only as good as what is best in the society. A shabby society ennobles shabby leadership. There are limits to a leader's ability to impose, or even persuade a constituency to accept, an agenda that is widely at variance with its thinking. This fact suggests that, on some levels, constituents consent to leadership; it is not forced on them.

Let us pursue this idea. Our society has many laudable features. There are many praiseworthy aspects of our world, but we also have less attractive dimensions. For example, we are willing to close our eyes to the poor, to the homeless. We are willing to ignore human pain and suffering. We cooperate in enshrining mediocrity at the expense of quality. We have embraced corruption by ignoring it, rather than eliminating it. We have produced an urban-dominated world that is increasingly antihuman—a society of the inarticulate, the uninformed, and the angry. Which features—the laudable, or the less attractive—does our leadership reflect?

Where does this leave us with regard to our expectations of leadership? We acknowledge societal influences, but this acknowledgment does not preclude forthrightness about societal needs. We urgently seek a value context for leadership that can be a declaration of opposition to the inferior in our society. We need a clear commitment to ensuring the cultivation of quality in intellect and thought. We need to reestablish a balance between public and private interests. Leadership needs to be a purposeful statement of sensitivity to human worth. Leadership makes a difference; the issue is to recognize how. Leadership is a series of important messages conveyed through decisions and demeanor.

All of this must be done with care; most leadership is subject to punishment in our society. One may exercise power, but not too much, and not with too much pleasure. Most college presidents walk a psychic tightrope, trying to be both effective and nonthreatening. Leadership is like love. We cannot define it or teach it, yet we can always identify it. We know when it is present and when we need it, but we cannot ensure its expression or perpetuation. We want it, and we reject it. Some leadership is like marriage, based all too frequently on compromise: Neither party gets all of what he or she wants. Some leadership is like divorce, with three sides to the story: his side, hers, and the truth.

In the main, leadership has a profound impact through its style. The dimensions of leadership behavior communicate more about a leader than most of the pronouncements or opinions that may be offered. Style is what constituents and peers see and hear. Style is what persists in the perceptions of those who surround a leader. Consider attention: Where does a leader direct it? Language: How does a leader use it? Sanctioning: What is a leader's attitude toward policy, moral issues, law? Personal demeanor: How does a leader carry himself or herself? Is he or she genuine? distant? warm? aloof? available? What about self-awareness? What sense does a leader have of the values conveyed by his or her behavior? Style is loud, clear, and public. A leader cannot hide it, explain it away, or be free of it.

If we lead by constant compromise and negotiation, if we lead by ignoring the obvious decay of our spirit and our strength, then we reflect what is worst in our society. This is not to argue that we will end the world's problems through leadership, but it is to acknowledge the centrality of leadership in ensuring the dignity of individuals, of our institutions, and of society.

Reference

Bloom, A. *The Closing of the American Mind: How Higher Education Has Failed Democracy and Impoverished the Souls of Today's Students.* New York: Simon & Schuster, 1987.

Judith S. Eaton is president of the Community College of Philadelphia.

Essential elements of college or university leadership are a passion for the institution, a commitment to stewardship, a clear but far-reaching vision, and the courage of one's convictions.

Essential Ingredients for Success

James H. Daughdrill, Jr.

In choosing a house, real-estate agents say, location is all that matters. In selecting a college or university president, search committees see leadership as the decisive factor.

It is very difficult to define the quality of leadership. Admittedly, colleges and universities demand many qualities of their presidents that are essential to the effective running of the academic enterprise. The list ranges from an ability to lead people and balance the budget to the capacity to make five speeches in two days and remain unruffled. Still, if one were to poll one hundred people on one hundred different campuses and ask them to name the most important presidential trait, my guess is that leadership would be their choice.

Leadership is a unique amalgam of attitudes and skills. It reflects the personality of the leader. Churchill was different from Gandhi, and John Kennedy was different from Harry Truman, but all four were effective leaders.

For me personally, what we call *leadership* is a mix that requires different talents at different times. Even so, there are four major ingredients that I believe are essential to the leadership of a college or university: a passion for the institution, a commitment to stewardship, a clear but far-reaching vision, and the courage of one's convictions.

J. L. Fisher and M. W. Tack (eds.). *Leaders on Leadership: The College Presidency.*
New Directions for Higher Education, no. 61. San Francisco: Jossey-Bass, Spring 1988.

Passion

When I was in my late twenties, I became president of a carpet manufacturing company with several plants in Georgia. I enjoyed my work and grew to like the trappings of corporate life. My real aspiration, however, was to retire at forty and go to work for a cause that meant something to me and earn only a dollar per year. Although it was mentally stimulating and financially rewarding, my work did not demand 100 percent in the "feeling" category. Certainly, I cared about our employees, the quality of our product, and the profitability of the operation, but I was not emotionally wedded to my organization in the same way I am now.

I believe being the president and leader of a college or a university demands a stronger concentration of feeling and passion than is true in business. To me, a college presidency is a calling much like that of a minister. It requires a love for the institution, its history, traditions, people, ideals, and values. It is a passion that consumes one's thoughts, fills one's dreams, invades every moment, and shapes every conversation. It is an emotion that cannot be faked. The president is simply too visible to mask true feelings for long.

This love for the institution comes before self. True leaders do not define their work in career terms, for a career implies a self-orientation that is antithetical to great leadership. They must be willing to subordinate their own desires to the needs of the institution. They must be willing to lose themselves in the institution, fight its battles, foster its values, and advance its goals.

This love is not perfect, unending, or complete. Every leader I know hates certain aspects of the job. What joy is there in a termination, or in the petty skirmishes that plague any community of bright individualists? Even leaders do not love every person all the time or relish every decision they are forced to make. Still, they must keep the embers of passion burning to sustain them when times are discouraging, frustrating, or lonely.

An enduring and consuming love for the institution affects not only the leader's ability to lead but also everyone else's ability to work together. In the literature on leadership, much is written about charisma. I believe that charisma is contagious love. Only if an individual possesses this passion or love for the institution can he or she effectively ignite this emotion in others, inspiring their support and commitment to the educational enterprise.

Stewardship

Experts on leadership cite numerous qualities that a leader must possess. They seldom single out personal stewardship, but they should.

When college presidents are honest, they concede that excellence in education depends on money. Because they may be uncomfortable talking about it, they may conjure up euphemisms like *resources* or *development* to avoid using the word—but what they mean is money.

The college president is more keenly aware than anyone else, on campus or off, that excellence is money-driven. He or she may camouflage this fact by saying that ideas, not money, drive the institution; but these words barely hide the reality: Money hires the thinkers. Furthermore, it keeps them. College presidents must come to grips with this fact, no matter how hard they may wish to change it.

I am occasionally asked by faculty members, "How in the world can anyone ask others for money?" The questioners certainly appreciate the benefits that money can bring—well-equipped laboratories, library collections, or time off for professional development. In such individuals' eyes, the means to those ends are painfully distasteful, but no college president can embrace that attitude. Indeed, a college president must have a personal philosophy about giving, a commitment to the concept of stewardship that transcends fundraising. Otherwise, he or she cannot, with integrity, ask others to support the institution in any significant way.

One of the oldest practices in the Judeo-Christian tradition is tithing. I have known many people who practiced prayer, meditation, or contemplative reading and eventually "fell off the wagon," but I have never met a person who stopped tithing of his or her own accord. There is something graceful about tithing. Skeptics may deride it as legalism, or as a long-outdated pretaxation ethic. Anyone who has ever tithed or given substantially, however, knows the powerful effect it can have on one's life.

In a society that equates happiness with ownership—a VCR in every den, a Volvo in every garage—philanthropy is increasingly viewed as a win-lose proposition, a zero-sum game that the giver loses. That is not true: When someone is asked to give a significant gift, something important happens, not just to the would-be recipient but also to the giver. The request for a significant gift may mark the first time someone has been asked to look beyond an acquisitive life-style. People spend lifetimes accumulating and then protecting what they have amassed. Until someone—say, a college president—asks for a significant, life-changing, values-questioning gift, few people ask, "How much is enough?" One of the basic needs of humankind is to give. Paving the way for an individual to meet that need is one of the greatest services to be offered.

Vision

The leader's function is to be a generalist in a community of specialists, organizing the specialists around a vision that gives focus and meaning to the common enterprise. The most important job of a leader is to have a dream that is in some way ennobling, to state it precisely and repeatedly, and to interpret this vision to others who can achieve it by working together. Vision unites and inspires the enterprise and motivates its people. If you consider the many leaders throughout history, in almost every instance you can state their visions or their dreams in a sentence or two. More important, those leaders could do so, too.

My first lesson on the wisdom of simplicity came from a friend of mine who was president of Coca-Cola. Our classroom that day was a football stadium; I was his guest for a Georgia Tech game. During the game, he explained that Coca-Cola had done considerable research on its soft drink and learned that Coke was viewed as a refreshment, while coffee was considered a mealtime drink. The company decided to change that image and set a target of capturing 3 percent of the national coffee market. Coca-Cola did it with a simple but effective slogan—"Things go better with Coke"—and an advertising campaign that pounded that message home. Those five little words broadened Coke's future.

At Rhodes College, our vision of ourselves as one of the finest liberal arts colleges in the nation has given us focus and direction. It is easier to reach a destination if one knows where one is going, and at Rhodes, everyone—students, faculty, staff, trustees, and alumni—has a plan and refers to it frequently. This vision is part of our collective consciousness. It shapes the thoughts, actions, and plans of those who live and work at the college.

Courage

Once the vision is stated, the leader becomes a kind of shepherd to the dream, a passionate advocate for the common effort. The leader must have the conviction to see that the original vision is not unnecessarily changed by the whims of fashion or tarnished by the immediate problems of the day.

The leader must at times be harsh, saying no to mediocrity. Others may compromise ideals, be indecisive, or try to be popular in every situation; the leader may not. The leader must be flexible, tolerant of mistakes by creative innovators—creativity accelerates institutional progress and must be encouraged at every opportunity—but intolerant of mediocrity.

The leader should maintain a vital distance between the day-to-day decisions of the college and the overall direction of the institution. This does not mean that the leader should become a recluse and ignore the pressing realities of the moment; it simply means that the leader is not always the one who should plunge headlong into administrative details that surround the running of a college or a university. There will, of course, be plenty of times when, because the institution's values are in some sense involved, the leader will need to step forward and make a firm decision on an otherwise inconsequential matter. Most of the time, however, such decisions are best handled before they reach the president's office.

The majority of decisions made by truly effective leaders are going to be the close calls, the tough decisions, simply because only the tough problems are going to make it all the way to the chief executive's desk. To make these decisions, a healthy dose of courage and self-assurance is required.

Any definition of leadership reflects the attributes and skills of the leader in question. My own definition is based on leadership positions in private business and in the church, as well as on the fifteen years I have served as a college president. Other leaders would frame different definitions out of totally different sets of circumstances and talents. No matter how different the recipes for successful leadership are, however, one indisputable fact remains: The best and most effective leaders would not trade places with anyone else in the world.

James H. Daughdrill, Jr., is president of Rhodes College, Memphis, and chair of the Association of American Colleges.

The most effective college presidents are those whose leadership styles are dominant, decisive, and, when appropriate, autocratic.

Conditions for Effectiveness

Jeanette T. Wright

Both leadership and management involve the ability to organize and motivate others to achieve common objectives. Therefore, a college president needs to excel in both leadership and management skills. It does not matter how well a president leads if resources and people are not managed properly; in such a situation the president will fail, and the institution will suffer.

Since leadership style is a function of the leader's personality, effective presidents possess leadership styles natural to them and appropriate to their particular organizations. The leadership style most appropriate to a particular organization is contingent on the organization itself. Many college presidents seem to perceive a college as a democratic organization and endeavor to lead by consensus. Educational institutions are highly structured organizations, with a variety of constituencies; and, in spite of their inherent academic freedom, liberal education, and ideals, they are in no respect democratic organizations, as any student will concur.

The educational and experiential backgrounds of college presidents vary, but the most common professional experience leading to the college presidency is that of academic dean (essentially an educator with administrative experience). The academic dean functions as "first among equals" with his or her colleagues and tends to move to the presidency with a democratic, egalitarian leadership style in the collegial environment.

J. L. Fisher and M. W. Tack (eds.). *Leaders on Leadership: The College Presidency.*
New Directions for Higher Education, no. 61. San Francisco: Jossey-Bass, Spring 1988.

88

I believe the most effective college presidents are those whose leadership styles are more dominant, more decisive, less democratic, and, when appropriate, autocratic. It is essential to listen to and encourage the ideas and opinions of others, but it is equally important to make one's own decisions and to be tough when necessary.

An Active Role

The role of the college president, who always serves at the pleasure of the board, is to be responsible for implementing policies prescribed by the trustees. Surely this is the essential role, but it is not a passive one. The leadership of a college is not vested in the board of trustees, but rather in the president. The president must possess a keen understanding of where the college is in its history, and a vision of what it can become— of what it will be, could be, or should be in the future. The president should envision a grand design. Every individual or group who has founded a college or a university has had a dream and perceived the need for an educational institution with a specific mission that called for deep commitment. Presidents, too, should possess the same intensity of commitment to take the institutions they serve from the present into the future.

Trustees are not educational specialists, nor do they invest large portions of their emotional or intellectual energies in the institutions they serve (compared, at least, to the investment they make in their own professions, businesses, and careers). The president is the one who has the obligation to share his or her visions and dreams for the college, and to inspire, inform, and given direction to trustees, who are in turn obliged to accept, modify, or reject the president's ideas. A president who has the respect and support of the trustees can and should exert influence on the philosophy of the college, its mission statement, and its short- and long-range plans. When the board reaches consensus, all policies should follow in that context and should be implemented by the president, with the full support of the board.

The exercise of power is an essential element of effective leadership, and the board of trustees vests power in the president. Effective presidents never forget either the source or the fact of their power, and they exercise it appropriately. There are two basic ways in which a president loses power. In the first case, the trustees, justifiably or unjustifiably, lose confidence in the president. Unless the president can regain or restore the confidence of the board, he or she should resign, because it is impossible to succeed without the board's support. Too often, presidents, in their sincere but impossible endeavor to satisfy all constituencies of the college at all times, forget that the board is what the president actually serves. In the second case, the president fails to exercise the power of the office: When there is not strong leadership, the power vacuum will inevitably be filled by an individual or a group in the college, and the president will lose control. College presidents should never allow themselves to be entrapped by personal, family, or economic needs that make resignation impossible. One should never need the job so much that one's values, ethics, or convictions will be compromised.

Belief in the Mission

Presidents cannot lead effectively if they are not committed to the philosophies or missions of the colleges they serve. Presidents have to believe profoundly in the intrinsic value of their colleges. This belief in the institution, intellectually and emotionally, is contagious and will enable successful leadership. It will also sustain the president during difficult and frustrating times, which cannot be avoided. When the president makes all decisions with the institution's philosophy and mission in mind, leadership will be consistent. Subordinates, too, should make decisions in the same way.

A college president must be strongly motivated by the desire to make a positive difference in the lives of others and less motivated by the desire for personal achievement or popularity. To be effective, the president needs respect but should not need approval. Over time, a president develops a thick skin and becomes less sensitive to criticism from members of the faculty and staff. Presidents must possess self-confidence, because they are constantly being evaluated and second-guessed by others.

The president must be a risk taker who is sometimes willing to be controversial. Especially during turbulent times, the president must take a stand. The president must possess moral character, a sense of humor, a sincere affection for people and especially for students, a persona that sets him or her apart from others, the courage to be different, and a high level of energy.

Alertness to Trends and Changes

The president must be aware of changes locally, nationally, and globally. He or she must be able to see trends and changes in the economy, governmental affairs, legislation, labor relations, the work force, society, and education. Then he or she must be capable of interpreting the effects these trends will have on the specific institutional environment. The president must interpret the need for institutional change and set the process of change into motion. The president must also have a sufficiently general understanding of current law to prevent lawsuits against the college; of course, legal counsel should be sought, as necessary.

Strategic marketing skills are important. The effective president needs to understand both the marketplace and the institution's market and to know the strengths and weaknesses of institutional competitors. Small colleges depend primarily on tuition, and steady enrollment is essential to their financial stability and solvency. At these colleges, it is common practice for the director of admissions to report directly to the president.

The importance of selecting talented administrators cannot be over-emphasized, and the president must replace them as quickly as possible when they do not perform to expectations. The president must delegate authority to others. When events prove others' decisions correct, the president should praise them generously. When errors are made, the president should assume most of the blame, because he or she is ultimately responsible. The president should be technically competent in most areas of responsibility and should appoint administrators who have expertise in specific areas.

At a small college, it is especially important for the president to be friendly and to show interest in all college personnel; social distance should be maintained, however. It is likewise important to demonstrate sincere, respectful regard for the needs and concerns of all personnel and to show trust and confidence in them. Reinforcement through praise and appreciation for work well done cannot be overemphasized.

Above all, an effective president has to love the job, with all its various roles, tasks, and activities, both on campus and in the community. To bring one's best to the position, with its long hours, evenings, and weekend commitments, and to endure the daily stress and frustrations, one must derive pleasure and satisfaction; otherwise, the presidency is not worth the sacrifices of personal and family life.

Postscript

The views, impressions, and attitudes about presidential leadership expressed here are derived from a love relationship of over thirty years with one small, private, two-year women's college—for the major part of my professional life. My first encounter with the college was my appointment as a part-time psychology instructor. Two years later, having been promoted to dean of the college, I was privileged to be able to make substantive changes in the philosophy and direction of the college with the full support of the founding president. During the nineteen years that followed, I served two more presidents, as academic dean and, later, as vice-president for academic affairs. I was then promoted to president and have served for nine years. Every morning as I drive onto the campus, my appreciation of its beauty and my pride in this college persist. My enthusiasm remains for the challenges, the resolution of new problems, and the surprises that each day inevitably holds. Commencement is the high point of every year for me, as another class of young women leaves the college better prepared for life and independence, their lives enriched by their experiences here.

Jeanette T. Wright is president of Bay Path Junior College, Longmeadow, Massachusetts.

Leaders must take advantage of opportunities for change, know
when to act and when not to act, have faith in their own
judgment, take risks, and enjoy building their institutions.

Nothing Worthwhile
Without Great Effort

Robert L. Hess

When I first assumed the presidency of Brooklyn College of the City
University of New York, I received conflicting advice from all sides. Some
colleagues warned that there was only one safe way to take on a new
administrative role: Study the situation for a year before acting. Others
admonished me to act before the institution swallowed me up: Strike
while the iron is hot. Some advised me to leave the faculty alone with
their prerogatives and focus on the institution's external relations. One
respected faculty member strongly urged me to develop a faction of sup-
porters within the faculty and not regard the entire faculty as a single
constituency. No one suggested that I look at the intellectual life of the
institution, become involved in curriculum development and evaluation,
or develop some sense of community on our commuter campus. No one
advised me that, as president of an urban public institution, I might
seriously involve myself in fundraising efforts, alumni affairs, intercolle-
giate athletics, construction of student housing, and public relations. All
concerned were wary about relationships with students after the stormy
administration-student interactions of previous years. I did not find the
existing literature on leadership or on the college presidency to be particularly helpful. I had no mentor. I was on my own. I quickly learned the
meaning of the college's original motto, *Nil sine magno labore.*

J. L. Fisher and M. W. Tack (eds.). *Leaders on Leadership: The College Presidency.*
New Directions for Higher Education, no. 61. San Francisco: Jossey-Bass, Spring 1988.

The college to which I came in 1979 defied easy description. In the days before New York City pressured the City University of New York to undertake a massive experiment in open admissions, it had enjoyed a regional reputation for excellence in the liberal arts and for the quality of its student body. The open-enrollment era seriously damaged the institution's reputation in the local community, even though our demoralized faculty had never been of higher quality. Old guard faculty perceived the college as essentially a liberal arts institution, but it was virtually a university in its own right. Nevertheless, the campus as a whole knew nothing about our very strong programs in the fine and performing arts, paid no attention to the potential importance of the school of education, felt threatened by students' demands for career-oriented majors, and prematurely lamented the demise of the liberal arts. Departmental chairpersons, competing for scarce resources, used the jargon of the higher education technocrats and spoke jealously of their FTEs, but not zealously of their academic programs. The college had lost its sense of mission. The administration had become the scapegoat for everything that had gone wrong, both in American higher education and at Brooklyn College.

The first major decision I made was not to choose between studying the situation at leisure and striking while the iron was hot. I determined that the college had to witness a number of visible short-term accomplishments so that I could buy time for the development of long-range plans. I had a plan for what I wanted to achieve during my first five years at the college, and I realized that both campus morale and my own credibility depended on my ability to produce some immediate and visible changes. I proceeded to lavish much attention on the campus's long-neglected physical setting, concentrating on the most heavily used public areas, in an attempt to indicate that change was possible. Graffiti disappeared, trash and garbage were collected, an ugly "temporary" building was torn down, and the main quadrangle was spruced up. These short-term accomplishments set a tone, established an initial track record, and showed the entire community that we were serious about reversing "deferred maintenance" (a euphemism for decay) and changing the campus environment, both physically and symbolically. Hope was again possible.

The second major decision was not to leave the faculty alone with their prerogatives. A full-scale faculty debate on general education reached its peak at the end of my first semester at the college. What was proposed in concept—a core curriculum—intrigued me, but the specific proposal fell far short of what it might have been. As president, I felt my major responsibility was to make sure that the faculty rose to the fullest and met the challenge of developing new graduation requirements. I was more aware than they were of the developing national concern for the quality of undergraduate education. When the time came, I spoke to the faculty council (of which I am not a member) on behalf of the concept, but in opposition to the specific proposal, which had been two years in the making. The proposal was defeated, to the consternation of all.

In the aftermath, a faculty delegation visited me to determine where I really stood. The opportunity then arose to present my conditions for support: new design of all courses (none to be simply repackaged), recognition of the need to incorporate cultural pluralism and newer areas of studies into the core curriculum, computer literacy, and a core that would not exceed roughly one-third of the course requirements for the baccalaureate. To make these conditions attractive, I offered a series of incentives for faculty development and for publication of curricular materials. I later revived a long-dormant humanities institute, as a catalyst and stimulus for the intellectual life of the campus. It became clear to me that, despite the constraints of a campus governance that gave faculty ultimate authority in curricular matters and a faculty ethos that excluded administrators from all such discussions, presidential leadership on campus must have both an academic and an intellectual component.

Once it was evident that new and universal general educational requirements would be developed by the faculty, I moved quickly to establish a task force on the future organizational structure of the college. Thus, my third major decision was not to keep an administrative structure that had been appropriate to an earlier decade. After public hearings and extensive debate among the college's various recognized governance bodies, I presented my organizational plan, which eliminated whole levels of campus bureaucracy. The change took effect at the end of my first year of tenure.

Still another dimension of that early period of leadership was provided by the student government, which had a long tradition of autonomy. No provision whatsoever existed for intervention by the college administration when dissension among the component parts of student government threatened the peace of the campus, especially when the very legitimacy of a student government action (passage of the budget) was challenged by members of the minority party in the student assembly. Strong divisions along racial and ethnic lines threatened to get out of hand. Faced with a resurgence of the racial tensions that had characterized the campus a few years earlier, I was determined to nip the problem in the bud. First, I placed a freeze (not a veto) on the expenditure of student funds. Then, in a heated four-hour meeting that I convened in my conference room before the students could organize a sit-in at my office, I told the student leaders that they would have to present their conflicting claims to the board of trustees, of which the student government was a creature, and not to the president. The board upheld the college administration, despite considerable trepidation among staff lawyers that the students would take the college to court. That is precisely what happened: The matter was resolved when the court ruled that the college president had an obligation to act, even if the college's governance document was silent on the powers in such a situation. My fourth major decision, thus, was not to be a powerless bystander in areas of student affairs that transcended the question of the student government's autonomy.

Underlying all these decisions was my understanding and accepting that a college presidency is not a full-time job, in the sense of forty hours a week. Days began at 7:00 or 7:30 A.M., when I could read the mail without being interrupted by insistent telephone calls, digest reports without being buzzed for my next appointment, or just quietly plan for the events of the day, the week, or the semester. Clearly, it would have been very easy to get so caught up in daily events and meetings that there would have been no time for thinking and planning. Therefore, I deliberately set aside time outside the whirlpool at the beginning of the office's (not the president's) day, and again after the secretaries had locked the office door behind them at the end of their day. College events and public events quickly consumed evenings and weekends; if my wife had not carefully guarded the hours reserved for family and personal renewal, I would have had no private life.

What lessons for leaders and leadership can be drawn from these highly personal experiences of the profession? There are no easy formulas. Each leader must have his or her own personal style, each set of circumstances must be handled in its own context, and each institution has its own traditions, but there are some generalizations I can make.

No matter how strong the traditions of an institution, change is inevitable; the question facing the leader is always only whether to be reactive or proactive. He or she must learn to know instinctively when to act and when not to act. The leader must be willing to explore unknown territory; he or she cannot fear the future. A heavy dose of optimism (or faith) is required. While no leader should act out of ignorance, neither should one be immobilized because not all the information is in (or not all pertinent data are available). This means, of course, that the leader must be willing to take risks.

As leader, the college president must capitalize on the opportunities for change as they present themselves. These may take many guises. First is the range of opportunities for physical or material improvement, which can have a significant psychological effect on the life of a campus. Then there are opportunities for institutional or administrative restructuring, which can relieve the campus of its bureaucratic burden (faculty should not have to worry about FTEs). Most important for the college or university are opportunities for intellectual, academic, and curricular excellence, which can release huge amounts of creative energy among faculty and administrators alike. The president who teaches on a regular basis (if only one course every three or four semesters) proves—in a unique form of hands-on academic leadership—that the educational experience is central to the institution. In this era after *in loco parentis*, one should also not overlook opportunities for establishing patterns of behavior that will lead to a better quality of campus life and improved human relations, especially as our student population becomes increasingly diverse. Finally, opportunities for publicizing an institution's successes bring the mission of the college into sharpest focus.

Not all change looks dramatic. Some change is dramatic only in its long-term impact. Changing the direction of an institution in a seemingly small manner can affect its ultimate destination, just as much as redirecting an interplanetary probe or an intercontinental guided missile by one degree can determine the success or failure of a mission. The leader must recognize that, by virtue of the very role of leadership, he or she is an agent of change. Moreover, if managing change is a fact of life for the leader, then the leader must recognize that tradition must also be prepared to resuscitate old traditions, break old habits, and create new traditions.

College presidents, as leaders, must enjoy building their institutions. That is their purpose; that is ultimately the measure of the quality of their leadership. They should not be working for personal aggrandizement. They have the rare opportunity to affect the lives of thousands, and in some cases tens or hundreds of thousands—indeed, even the life of a society. The college presidency also is a worthy end in itself; it should not be seen as a stepping-stone to some other career. To be most effective, however, the college president must have an extraordinary amount of self-control in budgeting time—not just for action, but also for reflection and planning; not just for the institution, but also for one's own human dimensions.

Robert L. Hess is president of Brooklyn College of the City University of New York.

To be a leader—a person who makes tough and meaningful decisions—one must be effective, and to be effective, one must have an inner sense of peace and security, as well as a vision for one's institution.

The Leadership of a University: Reflections

C. Peter Magrath

I hope there will be wisdom here for those who seek to define the essence of leadership and the responsibilities that go with being presidents—leaders, we would hope—of colleges and universities. I believe there is no one- or two-sentence definition of university presidential leadership. By definition, anyone who serves as a college president is a leader, if only in the narrowest institutional sense of having certain responsibilities to execute. Far beyond that, however, there are good, average, and bad presidents. The best are true leaders in one of our society's most difficult and exhilarating positions. I certainly have learned some lessons over the years, and one of them is that there is no single preferable leadership style. Even more important, leadership is highly contextual—flowing out of time, place, circumstances, and opportunities that are seized.

In reflecting on leadership and university presidencies, I find that four rules have worked for me. The first three are personal and speak to the inner person; live men and women, after all, serve as presidents. My fourth rule is more general and institutional.

Three Personal Rules

I start from the proposition that to be a leader—a person who makes tough and meaningful decisions—one must be effective. To be

J. L. Fisher and M. W. Tack (eds.). *Leaders on Leadership: The College Presidency.*
New Directions for Higher Education, no. 61. San Francisco: Jossey-Bass, Spring 1988.

effective, one must have an inner sense of peace and security. The personal rules based on this proposition are as follows.

1. *Want but do not need the job.* Men and women who do not want strongly to be university presidents ought not apply for, much less accept, such positions. It is tiresome and hypocritical to hear so often in the academic community the standard, too-modest disclaimer that the presidency has been thrust on one who suddenly must rise to the occasion and serve.

These jobs are for men and women who want them, who can accept both the joy and the pain that go with them and the many rays and shadows that lie in between. These jobs are for people who have visions they want to pursue on behalf of higher education and their colleges or universities. They are not jobs for the weak-kneed and the fainthearted, or for those who do not care about the exciting enterprise of learning and teaching.

Still, those who want these jobs must not need them. They must be men and women who—while enjoying the responsibility, the power, and the perquisites that go with these positions—do not feel that their ultimate personal well-being or their total persona is tied in with being "the president." They must know that the jobs are temporary, and that other mortals can just as well fill these positions.

Most important of all, from the first day on the job, they must have the attitude that they can leave it. They must feel that they can be independent of those for whom they work and to whom they feel the ultimate responsibility—whether these people are trustees, faculty, powerful alumni, or important political and governmental leaders.

It is not that university presidents should be indifferent to their boards, much less to the many constituencies and groups with which they must work; but they must not be beholden or sold out to anyone. If they are, they are incapable of asserting their true positions on issues and acting out of their most fundamental convictions. Moreover, the president who craves and needs the job above all else will be weak and ineffective. He or she will smell of both fear and indecision and, paradoxically, will therefore appear ineffective and useless to governing boards and to all others who want confident, strong presidents. The president must feel truly independent as a human being, as a person who can walk out if he or she must. Only then will the president be able to be strong, effective, and responsive. One should never threaten to resign, however. If you must resign, do so but do not threaten. That is not to say that one cannot make his or her deepest convictions and positions sharply clear to the governing board and to other authority figures. Any governing board worth its salt (and most of them are) understands and respects such clarity.

2. *Believe in your positions.* A university president must believe that any position or recommendation for which he or she works and

fights is the right one for the university. It may be the wrong position, of course; we are all fallible, and on tough issues there are excruciatingly difficult choices between positions that, at the margins, can go either way. Nevertheless, the president must believe that what he or she recommends is the right position and must work for it because it is in the best interest of the college or the university. If you do not feel that a position is right, you will not be effective in working for it.

An indispensable corollary to this rule is that presidents, regardless of how others feel, must feel the positions for which they work to be moral and decent, in spite of critics who may call the president immoral, weak, or cowardly. Your position may not necessarily be the right or the best one—by some standards, it may even be perceived as immoral—but presidents must, in their inner hearts and souls, believe that the positions they take are both institutionally right and morally compatible with their best judgments as human beings.

In over fifteen years as a university president, I have had to make some tough decisions and hard recommendations. Without question, they have not all been correct; certainly, some have been regarded as immoral by critics (usually single-issue critics).

Two decisions were particularly hard for me. As president of the University of Minnesota, I recommended that students have the option of seeking a refund on what had been a mandatory fee for support of the student newspaper, *The Minnesota Daily*. At times, that paper was a controversial (although provocative and useful) instrument of dialogue at the university. I made my recommendation because I believed that students should not be compelled to support a newspaper that at times took controversial editorial and other positions. Critics sharply disagreed with my position, believing that it had been politically motivated and that, in any event, it involved the actual or potential chilling of free expression among students and faculty. Eventually, after a lengthy legal process, a federal court ruled that the position was inconsistent with the first amendment. The regents, on my recommendation, decided not to pursue further litigation. As time passes, I can well say that perhaps my position was wrong, although even today it would be a close call for me. Still, I believed at the time of my recommendation (which my governing board accepted) that it was in the best interests of the University of Minnesota. Had I not believed that, I could not have made the recommendation, even as I can admit that my position may indeed have been wrong—and that under similar conditions today, I might well recommend otherwise. At that time, however, I also felt morally comfortable with my position. My morality is as questionable as that of any other human being, but in any such situation, we must be able to live with ourselves as individuals—with our true, inner selves—when taking controversial stands on issues that understandably agitate and trouble committed men and women.

The question of university investments in companies doing business in South Africa has been an equally complicated and difficult one for me. There are those who believe that the only right and moral decision is to make no investments in businesses operating in South Africa, but I do not see the matter that way. With equal fervor, however, I must concede that there is a strong and compelling argument for American universities to sever, at least for symbolic reasons, their investment ties with businesses still in South Africa. This is the position I have come to favor and to work toward. My point simply is this: Painful and bitter positions we take must reflect our best judgments of how to serve the interests of our universities.

What does all this mean? There are many tough and controversial decisions, but very few involve absolutely obvious questions of right and wrong. Presidents must always believe that the positions they are promoting and pursuing are right. If they do not believe that, both in their hearts and in their minds, they will not be effective presidents.

3. *Be firm but flexible.* Just as we do not want university presidents who are shrinking violets, afraid to make tough decisions, we also do not need presidents who cannot be firm and strong. Any good chief executive must take positions and hold to them; but it is possible to take positions in ways that are flexible enough to allow for change and adaptation as time, circumstances, and needs dictate.

If there is no ultimate wisdom and no ultimate right or wrong on many of the issues that come before university presidents, then a strong, secure leader can be open to change and adaptation. We do not need presidents who consult educational and political "meteorologists" on tough issues and change their forecasts, positions, and views from day to day. We do need men and women who are willing to listen, argue, and think; is that not the very essence of a university?

Style is equally crucial. There is no one correct style for leaders, but one fundamental point is true: If a president is personally secure, he or she can be strong and tough enough to admit that mistakes can be made, that positions need to be reevaluated, and that changes in direction are possible. Once again, we are back to the question of personal security and personal integrity, qualities of the inner man or woman who is called on to serve as president.

An Institutional Rule

My final rule is less personal; it is more official or institutional, and directed toward those who serve as college or university presidents.

4. *Have a vision.* There is no single plan or vision for a college or a university; our colleges and universities are wonderfully diverse and constantly face changing conditions and circumstances. Presidents are

their leaders, however, and leaders must have goals, vision, and a sense of direction for improving and changing the universities.

Without vision, there can be no direction, no improvement. Does anyone know of a college or a university that cannot be improved, both in what it is doing at the moment and what it aspires to do in the future? If a president does not have a plan for the university, why should he or she be president in the first place? It is much easier to coast and let the institution run itself; clearly, a great deal of what we all do is, inevitably, to maintain and conserve the enterprise. That itself is a very high and noble value, but every president who hopes to be an effective leader must have a vision and a plan for the institution.

Finally, let me tell you what leadership is not: It is not doing what single-issue persons want. So often over the years, I have been praised for making a tough, hard decision. I have been told, "You really exercised leadership on that issue." What the person was telling me, of course, is that I had made a decision he or she liked on a particular issue and that, therefore, I had exercised leadership. If I had made the opposite decision on the same issue, the same person would have told me that I had not exercised leadership and, worse yet, that I probably was immoral. We need to be a bit dispassionate about buying into the arguments of those who would push us one way or another for their special ends and interests. Often, too, a decision not made is just as hard and just as valuable as a decision to do something perceived as new, bold, and dramatic.

True leadership is not shown on any issue, much less on a single issue. True leadership is shown by chief executives who—day in and day out, on issues large and small—exercise their best judgment, consistent with their own moral values, of what serves the universities they are privileged to represent. That is leadership: It is making decisions by men and women who cheerfully, willingly, and without false modesty take stands, whether they are judged right or wrong by others, and who are open and accountable to the people they serve. It is hard work, but it is one of the most worthy enterprises that I can imagine.

C. Peter Magrath is president of the University of Missouri.
Previously, he was president of the University of Minnesota.

Index

A

Academic leadership, 5-8; and courage, 7, 8; and health of co-workers, 7; as moral leadership, 8; and morale, 7; and self-confidence, 6; and a sense of humor, 8; and vision, 5-8
Advice, 31-35; on ambition, 31-32; on choosing a compatible environment, 33-34; on commitment, 31; on enjoying yourself, 35; on knowing when to leave office, 34-35; on making decisions, 32-33; on recruitment, 32; on self-importance, 34; on using others' experiences, 33; on wanting to be president, 31-35
American Revolution, 10
Apprenticeship, 37-41; case for, 40-41; and coping with group dynamics, 39-40; and media image, 37-38; and tolerating anxiety, 37-39
Association of Governing Boards of Colleges and Universities, 63
Authoritarian approach, to presidential leadership, 76-77

B

Behavior of leaders, 77-79; and personal style, 79; and society, 78-79
Benchley, R., 59
Bennis, W., 33, 35
Bloom, A., 76, 79
Bowen, W., 32
Brooklyn College of the City University of New York, 93-97
Brown, D. G., 73, 74
Buena Vista College, 44-46

C

Cable Network News, 77
California State University, Long Beach, 51
Changing roles of college presidents, 71-74; in black colleges, 73; guidelines for success, 73-74; history and, 71-72
Character: and the college presidency, 47-51; and commitment, 48; and creating centers of excellence, 49-51; in decision making, 49; and risk taking, 51; and tenure-track appointment, 48
Chronicle of Higher Education, 1, 38
Civil War, 66
Coca-Cola, 84
College presidents as educators, 13-18; and the academic budget, 16-17; and clichés of the trade, 16; functions of, 17; and minorities, 17; and moral issues, 17; pressures facing, 13-14; and self-confidence, 15; and tenure, 14-15; versus as professional managers, 14
Collegial approach, to presidential leadership, 76-77
Commission on Strengthening Presidential Leadership, 63
Commitment, 3, 19, 31, 48, 81, 83, 89
Conflict, 53-58; and arbitrating third-party disputes, 57-58; knowing the outcomes of, 54-56; models of, 54-56; as a positive force for change, 54, 58; techniques for resolution of, 56-57
Courage, 2, 13, 15, 81, 84-85

D

Declaration of Independence, 10
Dignity: and the authoritarian approach, 76-77; and the college presidency, 75-79; and the collegial approach, 76-77; and individual freedom, 77; and leadership approaches and issues, 75-77; and leadership behavior and expectations, 77-79; and organizational freedom, 77; and personal style, 79; and society, 78-79
Dimock, M. E., 63
Djait, H., 12

N

A Nation at Risk, 11
National Commission on Excellence in Education, 11
National Commission on the Role and Future of State Colleges and Universities, 63, 64
Ness, F. W., 31, 35
Newman, F., 63, 64
Newsweek, 40
Nietzche, F., 18

O

Oberlin College, 59

P

Personal style, 3, 25, 79, 87, 96, 102
Presidential leadership, 99–103; an institutional rule for, 102–103; definition of, 99; and morality, 101; and personal style, 102; three rules for effective, 99–102; and vision, 102–103
Presidential service, 59–64; observations on, 59–60; and personal style, 60–61, 63; pitfalls of, 61–62; rewards and satisfactions of, 62–63
Princeton University, 15, 32

R

Rhodes College, 84
Riesman, D., 72, 74
Risk taking. *See* Character
Role models. *See* Apprenticeship
Rules for leadership, 99–103; on being firm but flexible, 102; on believing in the position, 100–102; on having a vision, 102–103; on wanting but not needing the job, 100

S

Saint Augustine College, 74
Self-confidence, 2, 6, 26, 89
Socrates, 17–18
South Africa, 102
Stanford University, 50

Strategic game playing: at a regional state university, 67–70; and industry, 68; and institutions, 66–70; and the marketplace, 69; and planning, 67–68; and the presidency, 65–70

T

Techniques for conflict resolution, 56–57
Terman, F. E., 50
The Third Man, 54
Thomas A. Edison State College, 32
Time, 40
Today's leaders, 9–12; and the average citizen, 11; and commitment, 12; difficulties facing, 10–12; and forces of modernity, 12; and history, 10; and opportunism, 10; and the U.S. Constitution, 9–10, 11–12

U

U.S.A. Today, 77
United States Constitution, 9–10, 11–12
University of Minnesota, 101
University of Notre Dame, 5–8, 34–35
University presidency: and ego, 26; and extracurricular activities, 26–28; managerial aspects of, 26–27; and media image, 28; and national stature, 28; and personal style, 25; and presidential authority, 25; and presidents of the past, 23–24, 28; and research universities, 24–29; today, 24–29; varied demands of, 26–27
University of Texas, 15

V

Vietnam War, 17, 28, 59
Vision, 2, 5–8, 29, 32, 43, 45–46, 49, 51, 66–67, 81, 83–84, 102–103

W

Wheeler, J., 15
Whitehead, A.W.N., 72, 74
Wriston, H. M., 60, 64